Gold
EXPERIENCE

B1

Preliminary for Schools

Workbook
Skills
Grammar
Vocabulary

T0350560

Jill Florent
Suzanne Gaynor

Contents

24/7 teens

READING

1 Read the text quickly and choose the correct answer.

1 Christine lives in a _small quiet town_/_a big lively city._
2 Christine is _an unusual person/a teenager like many others._
3 In her free time she enjoys _watching films/walking._

My name is Christine Petit. I'm fifteen and I come from Gardanne. It's a small town in the south of France. The countryside is beautiful and in the summer the weather is usually sunny and warm. Some people think it's boring here, but really it's quite interesting. Some very interesting people live in Gardanne; for example, there are several artists and musicians.

Every Saturday there's a market in the main street. A lot of people come to buy meat, fruit and vegetables, as well as clothes and shoes. I'm keen on cooking, so I often buy fresh food at the market. I cook for my family once a week.

Most days after school I meet my friends in the café. We drink cola and talk. Sometimes we go to a friend's house and listen to music. I often go out walking at the weekend. I love walking but I'm frightened of big animals. There are some horses in the field near my house, so I don't walk there. Gardanne isn't far from Marseille, a big city by the sea. Now and then I take the bus and visit friends in Marseille. We like watching the boats and walking around the old town. People from all over the world live in Marseille, so it's very lively and interesting.

I think I'm a typical teenager, and I live in a typical place. Many people live in towns like Gardanne. It's a calm place and there isn't a lot to do in the evening, but it's friendly.

2 Read the text again. Are the sentences (1–5) true (T) or false (F)?

1 Christine thinks Gardanne is a boring place. _F_
2 There is a market in Gardanne once a week. ....
3 Christine sometimes cooks for her family. ....
4 Gardanne is by the sea. ....
5 Christine thinks she's like many other teenagers. ....

VOCABULARY
Adjectives describing personality

1 Find twelve adjectives.

c	a	l	t	c	a	l	m	r
o	l	a	z	y	l	i	v	l
n	v	e	c	l	e	v	e	r
f	b	o	s	s	y	e	x	u
i	t	f	u	b	o	l	s	d
d	a	f	u	n	n	y	s	e
e	s	e	r	i	o	u	s	s
n	s	p	o	r	t	y	h	h
t	n	o	i	s	y	p	y	h

2 Match these words with the people in the pictures.

calm   clever   lazy   ~~noisy~~   shy   sporty

1 _noisy_   2 ....

3 _____   4 _____

5 _____   6 _____

3 Complete the sentences with the correct adjectives. The first letter has been given.

1 Amelia works hard and she's feeling c o n f i d e n t about her exams.

2 Dylan tells everyone what to do, he's b_____ .

3 Charlie is r_____. He doesn't say please and thank you.

4 Grace makes us laugh. She's f_____ .

5 Ethan doesn't joke or laugh. He's really s_____ .

6 Sophie always goes out and does lots of things. She's l_____ .

7 Julia always gets good grades. She's really c_____ .

8 Seb is a very c_____ person. He doesn't get nervous or stressed about anything!

4 Write the words under the correct headings.

| ~~bossy~~ calm clever confident |
| funny lazy lively noisy rude |

Positive	Negative
	bossy

5 Choose the correct prepositions.

1 We're excited *with/about/of* going to Rome.

2 Andy always wins. He's brilliant *at/of/with* playing tennis.

3 Don't worry, it's only a film. There's nothing to be frightened *with/at/of*.

4 We don't want Tony in the band. He's terrible *about/with/at* playing the guitar.

5 I'm really bored *at/with/in* watching TV. I want to go out.

6 John isn't interested *in/about/at* science. He wants to study history.

6 Complete the sentences. Use one or two words in each space.

1 James is ____*brilliant*____ at scoring goals.

2 We are _____ with doing boring things.

3 The children are _____ of the dark.

4 The students in my class are _____ about the school trip.

5 Chloe and Dan are _____ in geography.

6 Max is _____ at cooking. We can't eat the food he cooks.

7 Match the adjectives (1–6) with the prepositions (a–f).

1 brilliant   a with
2 excited   b about
3 terrible   c of
4 fed up   d in
5 frightened   e at
6 interested   f at

8 **Read the conversation and choose the best answer, A, B, C or D, for each space.**

Pat: Let's watch the rugby match between New Zealand and Australia.

Chris: You watch it. I'm not interested 1) ___*in*___ rugby.

Pat: Aren't you? I'm really excited 2) _____ it. New Zealand are brilliant 3) _____ rugby and I like the Haka, the 4) _____ dance they do before the match.

Chris: Are they doing the Haka now? Look! They're sticking out their tongues.

Pat: Yes, but they aren't being 5) _____ .

Chris: And they aren't laughing, they're very 6) _____ . Do you think the Australian team are 7) _____ of them?

Pat: No, I don't. The Australians are very good 8) _____ rugby.

Chris: My cousin is Australian. He's very 9) _____ , he plays cricket and he loves surfing and swimming, too.

1	**A** about		**B** in	
	C by		**D** with	
2	**A** at		**B** of	
	C about		**D** in	
3	**A** at		**B** in	
	C about		**D** by	
4	**A** sporty		**B** lively	
	C bossy		**D** calm	
5	**A** confident		**B** funny	
	C lazy		**D** rude	
6	**A** funny		**B** clever	
	C serious		**D** confident	
7	**A** interested		**B** bored	
	C excited		**D** frightened	
8	**A** in		**B** by	
	C at		**D** with	
9	**A** confident		**B** sporty	
	C funny		**D** shy	

GRAMMAR
Present simple and present continuous

1 **Write sentences and questions. Use the present simple.**

1 Where / you / come / from / ?
   Where do you come from?

2 Jacob / not / work in a shop

3 They / not / play football every week

4 Lily / like / ice cream

5 They / eat / rice every day / ?

6 Ethan / know / a lot of people here

7 Jacob / be / good at playing tennis / ?

8 All my friends / be / interested in music

2 **Complete the sentences with the present continuous form of the verbs in brackets.**

1 ___*Is Jo coming*___ (Jo / come) to the party with us?

2 Excuse me, you _____ (sit) in my seat.

3 What _____ (you / try) to say?

4 What _____ (you / do) now?

5 I _____ (go) shopping in town this afternoon. I need some new shoes.

6 It _____ (freeze) today.

7 The sun _____ (not shine) at the moment.

8 Tom _____ (not skate) on the lake.

9 Martyn _____ (not take) his exams this year.

10 _____ (we / meet) at 8 o'clock tonight?

3 Choose the correct words.

1 What _are you doing/do you do_ at the moment?

2 _I'm playing/I play_ a computer game.

3 _Is it snowing/Does it snow_ in the winter in your country?

4 It often _rains/is raining_ in tropical countries.

5 _I'm not understanding/I don't understand_ what you mean.

6 _He's coming/He comes_ from Russia.

7 _We're learning/We learn_ how to skate.

8 _She's wanting/She wants_ to stay at home.

9 They _don't study/aren't studying_ English this year.

10 _Does the sun shine/Is the sun shining_ now?

4 Complete the sentences with the correct form of the verbs in brackets.

1 Where ___does Aydin come___ (Aydin / come) from?

2 Makana _____ (love) living near the sea.

3 Millions of tourists _____ (visit) Hawaii every year.

4 We _____ (watch) the tennis. It's very exciting.

5 Andy _____ (not play) very well at the moment.

6 I _____ (not know) where my phone is.

7 It's always hot in tropical countries, it _____ (not snow) there.

8 What _____ (you / study) this year?

9 I'm just _____ (finish) this text to Pip and then I'll be ready.

10 Why do you meet up with friends if you _____ (spend) all the evening on your phone?

5 Complete the article with the best answer, A, B, C or D, for each space.

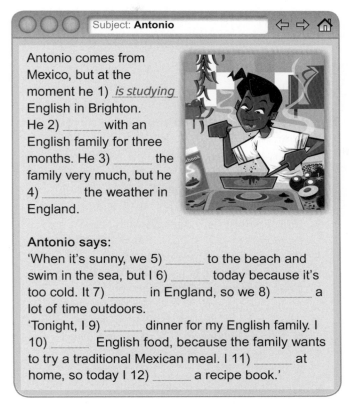

Subject: **Antonio**

Antonio comes from Mexico, but at the moment he 1) _is studying_ English in Brighton. He 2) _____ with an English family for three months. He 3) _____ the family very much, but he 4) _____ the weather in England.

Antonio says:

'When it's sunny, we 5) _____ to the beach and swim in the sea, but I 6) _____ today because it's too cold. It 7) _____ in England, so we 8) _____ a lot of time outdoors.

'Tonight, I 9) _____ dinner for my English family. I 10) _____ English food, because the family wants to try a traditional Mexican meal. I 11) _____ at home, so today I 12) _____ a recipe book.'

1 A studies   B is studying
  C doesn't study   D isn't studying

2 A stays   B is staying
  C doesn't stay   D isn't staying

3 A likes   B is liking
  C doesn't like   D isn't liking

4 A likes   B is liking
  C doesn't like   D isn't liking

5 A go   B are going
  C don't go   D aren't going

6 A swim   B am swimming
  C don't swim   D 'm not swimming

7 A often rains   B is often raining
  C doesn't often rain   D isn't often raining

8 A spend   B are spending
  C don't spend   D aren't spending

9 A make   B 'm making
  C don't make   D 'm not making

10 A cook   B 'm cooking
   C don't cook   D 'm not cooking

11 A usually cook   B 'm usually cooking
   C don't usually cook   D 'm not usually cooking

12 A use   B 'm using
   C don't use   D 'm not using

LISTENING

1 🔊 **1.1 Listen to Carmen and Piotr. Choose the things they talk about.**

1 school   4 weather
2 time   5 <u>books</u>
3 latitude   6 family

2 🔊 **1.2 Listen again and choose the correct answer, A or B.**

1 How old is Carmen?
  Ⓐ She's 16 years old. **B** She's 15 years old.
2 How does Carmen spell her surname?
  A S-A-N-C-H-E-Z **B** S-E-N-C-H-E-S
3 Which hemisphere does Carmen live in?
  A Northern **B** Southern
4 Does she live near the equator?
  A No, she doesn't. **B** Yes, she does.
5 Does Piotr live in a hot country?
  A No, he doesn't. **B** Yes, he does.
6 When does it get dark early in Piotr's town?
  A In the summer **B** In the winter
7 Who wears a coat in the winter?
  A Piotr **B** Carmen
8 Where does Carmen come from?
  A She comes from Poland.
  B She comes from Brazil.
9 Where does Piotr live?
  A He lives in Poland. **B** He lives in Brazil.

GRAMMAR
Time expressions

1 **Rewrite the sentences with the word in brackets in the correct place.**

1 We play football in the park in the afternoon. (usually)
  We usually play football in the park in the afternoon.
2 It snows in the desert. (never)
3 They laugh all the time. They are serious. (never)
4 We meet our friends after school. (often)
5 I get up early. (most days)
6 Is she rude? (always)

2 **Complete the text with these time expressions.**

every weekend	~~most days~~
now and then	once a week
twice a year	usually

💬 View previous comments   Cancel Share Post

I'm fed up with homework! I spend two hours doing
it 1) _____*most days*_____ and I have to complete a
project 2) _____. I really hate working
on Saturday and Sunday.
My favourite subject is drama. We have drama
lessons 3) _____, on Friday afternoon.
The drama group puts on a play
4) _____ – in December and June.
We 5) _____ perform a classical play,
but 6) _____ we write our own play.

Write a comment   Support

3 **Write sentences and questions. Use the present simple or present continuous.**

1 What / you / usually / do / after school / ?
  What do you usually do after school?
2 They / often / speak / Spanish / at home
3 It / rain / here. What / be / the / weather / like / there / ?
4 It / not / often snow / in the winter here
5 We / wait / for / the bus / to go into town
6 I / not enjoy / the party, so / I / go / home
7 Please / not interrupt / me / when / I / listen / to a programme
8 I / not watch / TV / because / I / cook / dinner

SPEAKING SKILLS

1 **Put the words in the correct order.**

1 your / ? / What's / name
 What's your name?

2 do / come / ? /Where / you / from

3 ? / do / live / you / Where

4 spell / do / name / you / your / ? / How

5 spell / ? / do / your / you / How / surname

2 **Read the questions. Match (1–6) with (a–f) to make answers.**

How do you come to school?
1 I come to school by bus, ___e___
What are you interested in?
2 I'm interested in art ___
What do you usually do after school?
3 I usually meet my friend after school ___
Do you enjoy learning languages?
4 I enjoy learning languages ___
What do you do in your free time?
5 I enjoy doing lots of different things ___
Do you think it's important to keep fit?
6 I think it's important to keep fit, ___

a for example, I'm learning to play chess.
b one reason is that we do our homework together.
c so I do lots of different sports.
d so I often visit the gallery at weekends.
e because I don't live near the school.
f because I have friends all over the world.

WRITING

1 **Choose the correct answer.**

1 It's winter now, *so/but* it's cold and snowy.
2 David isn't good at maths *or/and* science.
3 Susie works hard *because/and* she's confident about her exams.
4 Tony is rude *because/but* he makes me laugh.
5 Mary enjoys living in Barcelona *because/so* it's a lively, interesting city.
6 I have to study this evening, *so/because* I can't go to the concert.

2 **Complete the email with these words.**

~~and~~ but because or so

Hi, I'm Cecilia Ferradas, I'm fifteen 1) ___*and*___ I come from Santiago de Chile. I'm lively 2) _____ I'm not sporty. I don't like running 3) _____ swimming. People often think I'm serious 4) _____ I'm good at science. In fact, I enjoy making people laugh 5) _____ I'm not serious at all!!

3 **Read the notice about Pen Friends Worldwide and complete your profile.**

Pen Friends Worldwide
Make friends and improve your language skills!
Step 1: Complete your profile.
Step 2: Read people's profiles.
Step 3: Choose a friend and write them an email.

My profile
Name: _____
Age: _____
Nationality: _____
Personality: _____
Interests: _____
Language I'm learning: _____

4 **Write an email to a pen friend. Include your name, age, nationality, personality, interests and language you're learning.**

 **Hello? Hello?**

READING

1 **Read the text quickly. Which countries and languages does it mention?**

Countries: *Japan,* _____

Languages: _____

TRAVELLERS' TALES

Jessica went to Japan.

'I went to Tokyo to visit my friend Maki. I wasn't prepared at all. I didn't speak Japanese. I expected everyone to 1) *tell / talk / say / speak* English, but I was wrong! There was another problem as well – all the signs were 2) *by / at / in / with* Japanese. Some languages use the same alphabet as English, so you can recognise place names, but in Tokyo, I was lost! I couldn't read the signs and I couldn't ask for directions 3) *in / by / at / with* Japanese. How did I find my friend's house? Well, I found it 4) *on / by / for / to* accident. I knew she lived near the station, so I texted her when I came out of the station and she told me I was in her street, right outside her block of flats.

'Harry went to Kenya.

'I answered an advert for a voluntary job in Njoro. I was worried 5) *for / at / about / by* travelling alone because I didn't speak Swahili. How did I talk to people? Well, I met a lot of patient, friendly people. I bought a phrase book, and I used a lot of sign language. My Kenyan friends talked a lot, and although I didn't always know what they 6) *understood / translated / explained / meant*, I listened to what they said. They explained what they were talking 7) *about / for / at / in*, and they translated some of their conversations for me. I became more confident, and by the time I left, I spoke Swahili well. I made a lot of friends in Kenya, and I still talk to them.'

Isla went to Egypt.

'I had a wonderful trip to Egypt last year. Arabic uses, 8) *a same / an unusual / a special / a different* alphabet from English, so before I went to Egypt I learned a bit of the language. I found it easy to make friends in Egypt because I could speak a little Arabic. I talked to a lot of people and I didn't make too many bad mistakes. I knew a bit about the culture, too, for example, that people take off their shoes before going into someone's house, so I didn't walk into a house without taking off my shoes.'

2 **Read the text again. Choose the correct answer (1–8).**

VOCABULARY
Language and communication

1 **Complete the sentences with the correct language and communication words. The first letter has been given.**

1 Do you s *p e a k* Arabic?
2 Listen and I'll tell you how to p_____ this word.
3 Please can you e_____ what to do?
4 It isn't easy to t_____ poems from a different language.
5 Do you u_____ the text?
6 I didn't hear you. Can you r_____ that, please?

2 **Choose the correct words.**

1 *Listen/Hear*! This is important information.
2 What language do they *talk/speak* in Egypt?
3 I *understand/translate* Russian, but find it difficult to read.
4 Don't *say/tell* me the answer. I want to work it out for myself.
5 What did you *pronounce/say*?
6 Can you *repeat/tell* the words? I didn't hear the difference.
7 Let me *speak/explain* how to send a text message.
8 Do you *mean/say* you don't know or you won't tell me?
9 Sorry, I didn't *listen/hear* what you said – I was messaging my sister.
10 What did your parents *speak/say* when you told them your grades?

3 Complete the crossword.

```
        1 T                    2 M
3 P  R  O  N  O  U  N  C  E
4 U              5 S
                6 E        7 L
8 T
                           9 S
10 H           11 T
        12 R
```

Across

3 say a word with the correct sounds

4 know what something means

6 tell someone about something so they can understand it

8 to say things as part of a conversation

9 to speak words

10 to know that a sound is being made

12 to say or do something again

Down

1 change words from one language to another language

2 to have a meaning, definition or explanation

5 to talk to people; to say and understand words of a language

7 pay attention to what someone is saying or a sound

11 give information

4 Choose the correct answer, A, B, C or D.

1 Thank you for _____ me.
  A talking   **B** telling
  C speaking   **D** saying

2 Who were you _____ to on the phone?
  A hearing   **B** saying
  C telling   **D** talking

3 I'm sorry, I can't _____ you because it's too noisy here.
  A talk   **B** listen
  C hear   **D** tell

4 What did you _____ ?
  A say   **B** tell
  C talk   **D** listen

5 Do you want to _____ to music or watch a film?
  A speak   **B** listen
  C hear   **D** say

6 Do you _____ to your friends about your problems?
  A say   **B** hear
  C talk   **D** tell

5 Complete the sentences with *about* or *to*.

1 The teacher is speaking ___*to*___ the class.

2 She's speaking _____ learning languages.

3 She's telling them _____ her experience of living in different countries.

4 She's trying to explain the situation _____ them.

5 Are they listening _____ her?

6 Look, Holly is talking _____ Aiden. I didn't know they were friends.

7 What are they talking _____ ?

6 Match the sentence beginnings (1–6) with the endings (A–F).

1 I can't read the article aloud _D_

2 They speak very quietly _____

3 It's difficult to translate poetry _____

4 I want to remember the words _____

5 They didn't understand the first time _____

6 It's difficult to explain on the phone _____

A so I'm explaining it again.

B because the sound is as important as the meaning.

C because you can't see the picture.

D because I don't know how to pronounce the words.

E so I'm repeating them many times.

F so it's hard to hear what they're saying.

7 Complete the text with these verbs.

pronounce   repeat   say   ~~speak~~
translate   understand

💬 View previous comments   Cancel   Share   Post

Here I am in Beijing.
I'm travelling in China
for three months. I'm
learning to
1) _____*speak*_____
Chinese, but people
often don't
2) _____ what
I 3) _____ .
I use my hands a
lot, I point at things
and I 4) _____
everything several
times. Finally, I ask
my friend to
5) _____ for me. The problem is that I don't
6) _____ the words correctly. Chinese is a
very difficult language!

8 Replace the underlined words in the review with these words.

~~delicious~~   disgusting   fantastic   furious
hilarious   huge

Excelsior

Excelsior   **Overall rating: ***

The website described the food at the restaurant as
1) <u>very nice</u> 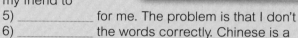 *delicious* , so we were expecting to
have a 2) <u>very good</u> 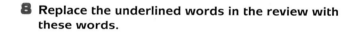 evening there.
We arrived at eight o'clock. The restaurant was
3) <u>very big</u> _____ and there weren't many
people there. We soon found out the reason.
The waiters mixed up the orders and brought us
the wrong things. At first, we thought it was
4) <u>very funny</u> _____ , but we stopped
laughing when we got the food. It was 5) <u>very bad</u>
_____ . Then we got the bill. The meal was
extremely expensive and we didn't think it was funny
at all. In fact we were 6) <u>very angry</u> _____ .

GRAMMAR
Past simple

1 Rewrite the sentences in the past simple.

1 Entering the talent show is a good idea.
   _____*Entering the talent show was a good idea.*_____
2 I am not confident about winning.
   _____
3 The prizes aren't very interesting.
   _____
4 This competition is a chance to change my life.
   _____
5 There are a lot of singers in the competition.
   _____
6 The other competitors aren't very friendly.
   _____
7 The judges are the most important people.
   _____
8 Are you the winner?
   _____

2 Complete the table with the past simple form of the verbs.

carry	1)	*carried*
come	2)	
have	3)	
move	4)	
plan	5)	
remember	6)	
study	7)	
win	8)	

3 Complete the text with the past simple form of the verbs in brackets.

Christopher Columbus

Christopher Columbus 1) _travelled_ (travel) from Europe across the Atlantic Ocean and 2) _____ (find) a new world. When he 3) _____ (leave) Spain in 1492, Europeans 4) _____ (not know) about America. Columbus 5) _____ (want) to find a new way to India. It 6) _____ (take) him five weeks to cross the ocean. He 7) _____ (not expect) to discover America. After their long journey, he and his men 8) _____ (believe) they were in India.

4 Write questions.

1 Amelia told Stephen about the party.
   Did Amelia tell Stephen about the party?

2 You visited England last year.
   _____

3 James worked in a Turkish restaurant.
   _____

4 James studied languages at school.
   _____

5 You went to the cinema yesterday evening.
   _____

6 You explained how to play the game.
   _____

7 They were at home last night.
   _____

8 It was a good idea to tell them about the trip.
   _____

LISTENING

1 🔊 2.1 Which methods did Lucy try when she was learning to cook? Listen and choose the correct answers.

1 She learned from her mother.
2 She watched TV cookery programmes.
3 She read a book.
4 She got an app.
5 She watched a friend.
6 She took a course.

2 🔊 2.2 Listen again and complete the notes.

1 Title of course: _Learning to Cook_
2 Length of course: _____
3 Number of students: _____
4 On the first day the students learned how to
   _____ .
5 On the final day, students had to _____
   with _____ courses.
6 Lucy had problems with _____ and
   _____ .
7 Lucy decided to cook _____ with
   _____ .

GRAMMAR
Past simple and past continuous

1 Complete the sentences with the past continuous form of the verbs in brackets.

1 I ___was studying___ (study) Turkish last year.
2 They _____ (tell) me about their home town.
3 He _____ (not speak) Spanish.
4 They _____ (not listen) to you.
5 Where _____ (Aiden / go)?
6 Who _____ (they / expect) to meet?
7 She _____ (watch) an interesting programme.
8 We _____ (not enjoy) the party.
9 Who _____ (you / talk) to?
10 They _____ (plan) to arrive by lunchtime

2 Complete the sentences with the past continuous form of these verbs.

~~cook~~   listen   play   send   take   watch

At four o'clock on Saturday afternoon,
1 Daniel ___was cooking___ pasta.
2 Harry _____ photos.
3 Max and Isla _____ chess.
4 Holly and Ella _____ to music.
5 Lily and Emily _____ TV.
6 Jacob _____ a text message.

3 Choose the correct words.

1 Columbus *tried/was trying* to find a new way to India when he *discovered/was discovering* America.
2 What *were they talking/did they talk* about when I *came/was coming* into the room?
3 They *didn't speak/weren't speaking* to us in Spanish while we *stayed/were staying* with them.
4 When we *arrived/were arriving*, all the guests *danced/were dancing*.
5 I *waited/was waiting* at the bus stop when I *saw/was seeing* the accident.
6 I *didn't use/wasn't using* my phone while I *travelled/was travelling*.

4 Complete the conversation with the correct past form of the verbs in brackets.

Granddad

Why 1) ___didn't you take___ (you / not take) a camera, a map or a guidebook on your holiday?

Ella

I didn't need them. I just 2) _____ (put) my smartphone in my pocket. When I 3) _____ (sightsee), I 4) _____ (use) my phone as a camera. When I 5) _____ (look) for somewhere to eat, my phone 6) _____ (become) a guidebook.

Granddad

I see! Your smartphone can do everything, so you 7) _____ (not carry) a heavy bag.

Ella

Right! That's why I 8) _____ (not get) tired when I 9) _____ (visit) different places.

SPEAKING SKILLS

1 Put the sentences in the conversation (a–f) in the correct order (1–6).

a Mia: Hang on. I'll go outside ... How's that? ....

b Dad: Oh, yes. OK, see you soon. ....

c Dad: Sorry, I can't hear you. What did you say? ....

d Mia: Hi Dad, it's me. I'm at the station. Can you come and get me? __1__

e Mia: OK. Can you come and get me please Dad? ....

f Dad: That's better, but can you speak louder? ....

2 Complete the sentences. Use one word in each space.

1 The line is very bad. What did you __say__? Can you repeat that, please?

2 It's very noisy here. .... a minute, I'll find a quiet place.

3 Oh dear, I was talking to Ava, but we were cut .... I'll try to call back.

4 I'm trying to call Noah, but I haven't got a .... I'll go outside and try again.

5 Hello? Is that Jacob? I can't .... you. Can you speak a bit louder, please?

WRITING

1 Complete the text with these words. Use the words in brackets to help you.

> beautiful   disgusting   furious   hilarious
> terrible   ~~wonderful~~

💬 View previous comments   Cancel   Share   Post

My friend Maki was very surprised yesterday when I took her to a 1) _wonderful_ (very good) Japanese restaurant and told her that I love Japanese food. She reminded me of the day that she took me to her home after school. Her mother and father were very kind and invited me to eat with them. That was the first time I tried Japanese food. Everything looked 2) .... (very nice), but when I put something in my mouth, it was 3) .... (very bad). I couldn't eat it, but I couldn't spit it out. What a 4) .... (bad) situation. I looked at Maki, and she understood. She took me into the kitchen where I took the horrible thing out of my mouth and threw it away. I started to cry, I thought Maki's parents would be 5) .... (very angry). Then Maki began to laugh, she thought it was 6) .... (very funny)!

2 Read the text and choose the correct answer, A or B.

1 When did the main event happen?
  A yesterday
  (B) one day after school

2 Where did it happen?
  A in a Japanese restaurant
  B at Maki's house

3 Who was there?
  A Maki's parents, the writer and Maki
  B Only Maki and the writer

4 What was the main action?
  A The writer took Maki to a restaurant.
  B The writer tasted Japanese food for the first time.

5 What happened in the end?
  A Maki laughed.
  B Maki's parents were angry.

3 Plan a story for the school magazine. Use these questions to help you make notes.

When did the main event happen? ....
Where did it happen? ....
Who was there? ....
What was the main action? ....
What happened in the end? ....

4 Write the story for the school magazine. Use your notes and write about 100 words.

Revision Units 1 – 2

VOCABULARY

1 Complete the descriptions with these words.

> about   at (x4)   in   ~~of~~   with

Ava

I'm frightened 1) _of_ speaking in public and I don't like parties because I'm not good 2) _____ talking to people I don't know. I prefer to listen to other people. I don't like to say what I think, in case people disagree with me.

Evie

I love playing tennis and football. I get excited 3) _____ competitions. I don't understand how people can sit still. I always want to run and dance. I love parties, I play the saxophone and I get fed up 4) _____ people telling me to be quiet!

Charlie

He works hard and gets good grades. He's interested 5) _____ learning new things and quick to understand new information. He is brilliant 6) _____ explaining things to his classmates, too. He likes organising people and telling them what to do.

Daniel

He enjoys making people laugh and is good 7) _____ telling jokes. He is bad 8) _____ listening in class, so he doesn't hear the teacher's questions. He doesn't apologise. He is often late for school and doesn't always do his homework.

2 Read the descriptions in Exercise 1 again and complete the sentences. The first letter has been given.

Ava is 1) s _h_ _y_ . She isn't 2) c_____ .
Evie is 3) s_____ and 4) n_____ .
Charlie is 5) b_____ .
He's 6) c_____ .
Daniel is 7) f_____ , but he's 8) l_____ .

3 Choose the correct words.

1 Please *hear/listen to* what I'm *saying/talking*.
2 Can you *explain/translate* what you *understand/mean*?
3 What did they *tell/speak* you?
4 How do you *pronounce/repeat* this word? I don't know how to *speak/say* it.
5 I don't *explain/understand* what you're *talking/telling* about.
6 Can you *speak/translate* this word? I don't know what it *means/pronounces*.
7 Can you *repeat/talk* that, please, I didn't *listen to/hear* you?
8 I enjoy *listening to/hearing* my grandfather *talking/telling* stories.

GOLD EXPERIENCE

GRAMMAR

1 Complete the text with the correct form of the verbs in brackets.

💬 View previous comments   Cancel   Share   Post

I usually 1) _____speak_____ (speak) Spanish at home, but today I 2) _____ (speak) English, because my friend from England 3) _____ (stay) with me.
He 4) _____ (come) to school with me every day, because he 5) _____ (learn) Spanish. There are a lot of words he 6) _____ (not know), so I 7) _____ (translate) the words and 8) _____ (explain) the grammar.
My English 9) _____ (improve), but his Spanish 10) _____ (not get) better!

2 Write questions.

1 What language / Felipe / usually / speak / ?
    What language does Felipe usually speak?

2 Why / he / not speak / Spanish today / ?

3 Why / Felipe's friend / stay / with him / ?

4 Where / Felipe and William / go every day / ?

5 Why / Felipe / translate / a lot of words / ?

6 Why / William's Spanish / not get / better / ?

3 Rewrite the sentences in the past simple.

1 Felipe and William are good friends.
    Felipe and William were good friends.

2 Felipe takes William to visit his friends.

3 Does William go to school with Felipe?

4 Felipe and William speak English all the time.

5 Why don't Felipe and William speak Spanish?

6 William doesn't speak Spanish very well.

7 Felipe translates the words William doesn't know.

8 William stops trying to speak Spanish.

4 Complete the sentences with the past simple form of the verbs in brackets. Put the time expressions in the correct place in the sentences.

1 We _____ (have) a holiday when I _____ (be) a child. (every year)
    We had a holiday every year when I was a child.

2 We _____ (spend) holidays at the beach. (often)

3 I _____ (go) swimming. (most days)

4 My parents _____ (buy) me an ice cream. (usually)

5 My sister and I _____ (find) interesting animals on the beach. (now and then)

6 We _____ (take) took them home. (never)

7 We _____ (be) happy to go to the beach. (always)

8 We _____ (play) beach games. (sometimes)

5 Choose the correct words.

Mountain Adventure
One day last summer my brother and I were walking in the mountains when the weather suddenly
1) **changed**/**was changing**. One minute it was hot and sunny, the next it 2) **rained**/**was raining** very hard. We were wearing T-shirts and shorts. We
3) **didn't have**/**weren't having** any warm clothes with us. We 4) **ran**/**were running** down the mountain to find shelter when my brother
5) **fell**/**was falling** over and hurt his leg.
While we 6) **tried**/**were trying** to call for help, we
7) **dropped**/**were dropping** our mobile phone and the screen broke. Luckily, our parents 8) **already came**/**were already coming** to find us. We were very happy to see them!

03 Sounds of the future

READING

1 Read the article quickly. Choose the items of home technology it mentions.

1 air conditioning
2 dishwasher
3 <u>microwave</u>
4 robot vacuum cleaner
5 fridge
6 washing machine

Smart technology – how will it change our homes in the future?

At the moment, some smart technology for the home is available, but it's expensive. When it becomes cheaper, it will be more popular – and it could change our lives.

First thing in the morning, your phone will wake you up. It won't let you switch off the alarm until you get up! Your phone will also control the lights and air conditioning, switching them off when you go to bed and on when you get up. The microwave will heat up your breakfast. The washing machine will send you a message when it's finished washing your clothes and the oven will let you know when your dinner is ready. The fridge will tell you what food you've got and send you a message when somebody takes something out. Then it will remind you what to buy at the supermarket. It will also suggest recipes for the food you already have.

Do we want technology to control our homes? We asked some teenagers how useful they think these gadgets will be.

Poppy – 'I hope my parents won't buy a smart fridge. The fridge will order the same food all the time, so we won't get to try new things. And I don't want a fridge that's going to send my mum a message every time I eat something. I don't want to feel that the house is watching everything I do.'

Thomas – 'I think smart technology is cool. It will help to reduce the amount of energy we use. We'll waste less food because the fridge will give us ideas for meals. I won't have to check when the washing machine finishes washing my clothes. I'll just wait for it to send me a message, and that's really useful. Technology is going to change our homes and I think that's a good idea. When technology does more of the boring things, I'll have more time to do the things I like doing.'

2 Read the article again. Choose the correct answer, A, B, C or D.

1 What is the article trying to do?
   A Persuade people to save energy.
   (B) Find out what people think about home technology.
   C Persuade people to buy a smart fridge.
   D Find out what home technology people use.

2 Why does the article say that smart technology for the home isn't popular?
   A It's too expensive.
   B It isn't available yet.
   C No one is interested in it.
   D It doesn't work.

3 What does the article say about your phone?
   A It won't let you stay up late.
   B It won't wake you up.
   C It will tell you what's in the fridge.
   D It will know when you go to bed.

4 What does Poppy say about a smart fridge?
   A She doesn't want one.
   B It will make meals more interesting.
   C Her mum will send messages to the fridge.
   D It will tell her when to eat.

5 What does Thomas think about home technology?
   A It will make us lazy.
   B It will make our lives more interesting.
   C It's boring.
   D It's not going to change anything

VOCABULARY
Technology around the home

1 Match (1–6) with (a–f) to make compound nouns.

1 air
2 dish
3 electricity
4 hair
5 head
6 washing

a dryer
b conditioning
c machine
d phones
e supply
f washer

GOLD EXPERIENCE

2 Complete the sentences with these words.

> fridge   hair straighteners   ~~iron~~
> microwave   plug   speakers

1 My shirt is clean and dry and now I need to use the _____*iron*_____ .
2 Let's use the _____ so we can all hear the music.
3 Put the butter in the _____ to keep it cool.
4 You can heat food quickly in the _____ .
5 Which _____ is for the computer?
6 I use _____ because I don't like my curly hair.

3 Answer the questions.

1 Where do you put dirty cups and plates?
   In the dishwasher
2 Where do you put food to keep it fresh?
   _____
3 What do you use to dry your hair?
   _____
4 What do you use to connect a machine to the electricity supply?
   _____
5 What do you use to keep a room cool?
   _____
6 Where do you put dirty clothes?
   _____

4 Complete the email. The first letter of each word has been given.

Subject: **My holiday!**   ⇦ ⇨ ⌂

Hi Grace
I'm on holiday in Spain. We're staying at a lovely house, but yesterday the 1) e*lectricity* s*upply* failed and all the machines in the house stopped working! I washed my hair, but I couldn't use the 2) h_____ to dry it. We couldn't heat any food because the 3) m_____ wasn't working and the food in the 4) f_____ went bad. We had to wash the plates by hand because we couldn't use the 5) d_____ . We haven't got anything to wear because our clothes are in the 6) w_____ m_____ and they're still dirty. I didn't know how much we needed electricity!
Hope you get this message!
Charlotte

---

5 Match the sentence beginnings (1–6) with the endings (A–F).

1 The pictures on *C*
2 I put my food _____
3 I use hair straighteners _____
4 I switched on the air conditioning _____
5 We used the microwave _____
6 Put your dirty plate _____

A because the room was very hot.
B in the dishwasher, please.
C our new 3D TV are great.
D because I don't like curly hair.
E in the fridge to keep it fresh.
F to heat our pizzas.

6 Choose the correct phrasal verbs.

1 Remember to *switch off*/turn down/plug in the lights when you go out.
2 Can you *turn up/turn down/switch on* the TV, it's too loud.
3 We can't get any more plates in, so please *switch on/turn up/plug in* the dishwasher.
4 Please *plug in/turn up/pick up* your dirty clothes and put them in the washing machine.
5 I need to *switch off/plug in/turn down* my hairdryer to dry my hair.
6 Please *pick up/switch on/turn up* the oven, it isn't hot enough.
7 *Switch on/Plug in/Switch off* the computer, we aren't using it now.
8 Don't *plug in/switch on/turn down* the washing machine, I want to put some more clothes in it.

7 Complete the crossword.

Across

4, 3 down   If a room is very hot, you need _____ .

7, 6 down   Use these if you don't want curly hair.

9, 5 down   Plug in the computer to connect it to the

  _____ .

12, 1 down Switch on the _____ to wash your clothes.

13   Keep food in the _____ .

14   Heat food in the _____ .

Down

1   See 12 across.

2   Wash and dry your clothes and then use the

  _____ .

3   See 4 across.

5   See 9 across.

6   See 7 across.

8   Use your _____ to listen to your MP3 player.

10   Turn up the _____ so we can hear the music.

11   Clear the table and put the plates in the

  _____ .

GRAMMAR
Talking about the future: will, going to

1 Put the words in the correct order to make sentences.

1   Technology / going / to / is / change / lives / our / .

    Technology is going to change our lives.

2   your / birthday / I'll / a cake / for / make / .

3   washing machine / Will / switch on / you / the / ?

4   to write / We / a shopping list / won't / need / .

5   will / The / fridge / text message / us / send / a / .

6   I'm / air conditioning / going / to / turn on / not / the / .

7   They / tomorrow / are / to / buy / new / a computer game / going / .

8   headphones / you / Are / to / buy / some / new / going / ?

2 Choose the correct words.

Lucy: What 1) <u>*are you going to*</u>/*will you* do at the weekend?

Mia: 2) *I'm going to/I'll* meet my friend Ella in town on Saturday. We plan to look round the shops.

Lucy: 3) *Are you going to/Will you* buy some new clothes?

Mia: Yes, I expect 4) *we're going to/we will*.

Lucy: Sounds great! 5) *I'm going to/I'll* come with you!

Mia: 6) *I'm not going to/I won't* take a lot of money, because I don't want to spend too much.

Lucy: I agree, 7) *I'm not going to/I won't* spend a lot of money, either.

Mia: OK, let's go together. 8) *Are you going to/ Will you* call me when you're ready to leave?

Lucy: Yes, and 9) *I'm going to/I'll* meet you at the station.

Mia: OK, 10) *I'm going to/I'll* buy the tickets.

3 Complete the sentences with the correct form of *will* or *going to*.

1 It's really hot in here.
OK, I *'ll*_____ turn up the air conditioning.

2 We can help you tidy up. We _____ put the dirty plates in the dishwasher.

3 Harry's hungry, so he _____ heat up a pizza.

4 When we get a smart fridge, we _____ run out of food.

5 What _____ (you) see at the cinema?

6 I _____ buy a new computer game tomorrow.

7 _____ (you) help me with my homework later?

8 _____ (Oscar) show us his photos tonight?

4 Complete the conversation with the correct forms of *will* or *going to* and the verbs in brackets.

Jake: Hi, Harry, where are you going?

Harry: To the computer shop.
I 1) *'m going to buy* (buy) a new game.

Jake: OK, I 2) _____ (come) with you.

Harry: The games are in order, so it 3) _____ (not take) long to find the one I want.

Jake: There are no prices on these games. I 4) _____ (ask) how much they cost.

Shop assistant: They're 10 euros today, but we 5) _____ (have) a sale next week, so these games 6) _____ (be) cheaper. They 7) _____ (cost) 8 euros.

Harry: Thanks! I 8) _____ (not buy) the game today. I 9) _____ (wait) until next week.

LISTENING

1 🔊 3.1 Listen to the speakers (1–5) and choose the correct answer, A, B or C.

1 Which of these things do the speakers decide is the most important?

A (B) C

2 Which of these items is not mentioned?

A B C

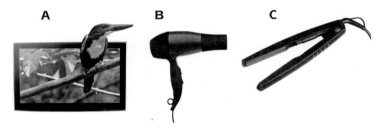

3 What does the girl want to do?

A B C

4 What do they need?

A B C

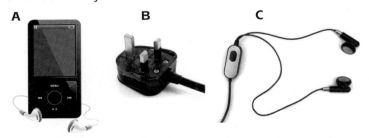

5 What are they going to eat?

A B C

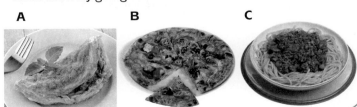

GRAMMAR
someone, anyone, everyone, no one, something, anything, everything, nothing

1 Rewrite the sentences. Replace the underlined words with a single word.

1 They didn't put <u>any of the things</u> in the drawer.
   They didn't put anything in the drawer.

2 We told <u>all the people</u> what to do.

3 I saw <u>a person</u> take your phone.

4 <u>None of the people</u> offered to help.

5 The cat pushed <u>a thing</u> off the shelf.

6 They used a lot of plates and cups and they left <u>all of the things</u> dirty.

2 Choose the correct words.

Subject: **Yesterday**

Hey Ava
You missed a fun event yesterday! I was at the shopping mall when I noticed that 1) <u>everyone</u>/someone/everything was waiting for 2) anything/nothing/something to happen. At first, 3) anyone/no one/nothing moved, then 4) someone/anyone/everyone began to dance and, one by one, we all joined in until 5) anyone/everyone/someone was dancing. Then, suddenly the music stopped, and 6) anything/something/everything was quiet again.
Why don't you come to the mall next Saturday?
Jake

3 Complete the sentences with these words.

anyone	anything	everyone	~~everything~~
no one	nothing	someone	something

1 Are you ready to start? Have you got ___everything___ you need?

2 There were a lot of people there, but _____ spoke to me.

3 We won't start until _____ is sitting down.

4 There's _____ missing, but I'm not sure what it is.

5 The room is locked. Does _____ have the key?

6 The box is empty, there's _____ in it.

7 I can't manage on my own. I need _____ to help me carry this heavy bag.

8 Are you hungry? Can I get you _____ to eat?

4 Complete the conversation. Use one word in each space.

Lily: We're going to have a party at the end of term.

Jessica: 1) ___Everyone___ in our class will be invited and we'll do 2) _____ ourselves.

Max: OK, I'll write the invitations.

Lily: Great! Make sure 3) _____ is left out.

Max: Has 4) _____ got a pen?

Lily: Next, 5) _____ needs to buy the food and drink.

Alfie: OK, I'll do that.

Lily: Thanks, Alfie. So, I think 6) _____ has got 7) _____ to do.

Alfie: Yes, that's right. Max is going to write the invitations. I'm going to buy the food and drink.

Max: Is there 8) _____ else to do?

Jessica: Yes, the music! I'll look after the music. I'll make sure there are songs that 9) _____ likes.

Lily: Great, now there's 10) _____ left to organise.

All: We're going to have a great time!

SPEAKING SKILLS

1 Complete the sentences with these words.

> be   good   ~~maybe~~   so   that's   sure

1 Well, ___maybe___ you're right.
2 I don't think _____ .
3 I think _____ right.
4 I'm not _____ .
5 You might _____ right.
6 That's a _____ point.

2 Put the sentences from the conversation (a–f) in the correct order (1–6).

a Grace: I don't agree! It sounds like a cat with a cold. ___
b Grace: Oh, but we won't know whose phone's ringing! ___
c Lily: Alfie's new ringtone is so cool. ___1___
d Grace: Hilarious?! It's not funny at all. ___
e Lily: Well, I like it. I'm going to get it too. ___
f Lily: Well, maybe, but I think it's hilarious. ___

WRITING

1 Complete the text with *a*, *an*, *some*, *the* or *x* when no word is needed.

> View previous comments   Cancel   Share   Post
>
> We know a good smell means 1) ___a___ good taste, but scientists have done 2) _____ experiment to show that 3) _____ sounds also change the way food tastes. The results of 4) _____ experiment are useful for food companies because they will be able to reduce 5) _____ amount of salt and sugar in food, and make it healthier. This experiment shows that 6) _____ food companies need to think about 7) _____ way food looks and the way it sounds. Companies now know that 8) _____ food packet that makes the right noise makes the food inside seem fresher, so they are changing the material they use for 9) _____ crisp packets.

2 Link the sentences with *and*, *because*, *but* or *so*.

1 Sugar and salt make food taste good ___but___ too much sugar and salt isn't healthy.
2 Sounds can change the way food tastes _____ companies are changing the material they use for crisp packets.
3 The crisps in the new packets seem fresher _____ the packets make the right noise.
4 Companies think about the way food looks _____ the way the packet sounds.

3 Write about food in the future. Answer these questions. Give your opinions and a reason or a result. Write about 100 words.

1 In ten years' time, will people eat the same food or healthier food?
2 Will more people buy ready-to-eat food?
3 What sort of packaging will food companies use?
4 How will the packaging affect the food we eat?
5 Will people have time to cook?

In ten years' time, I think people will …

READING

1 Read the first email only and answer the questions.

1 What do they want to find out?

_____

2 Who is going to learn a new skill?

_____

3 Who is going to teach a new skill?

_____

Hi Jess,
Everyone has to practise in the playground. It's too dangerous to skateboard in the corridors so there's a rule 7) *for / on / to / against* it. I think you're right that the students will find it easier than the teachers. In my opinion, the teachers are 8) *too / enough / to / as* old to learn skateboarding. I don't think they will be brave enough to go fast on the board! 9) *Addition / Also / As / Too*, the students will probably have more time to practise.
Paul

Hey Jess!
We're doing a really cool experiment at school to find out what's the best age to learn a new skill. I think it's going to be more fun than our usual science lessons. The idea is to teach four teachers and four students 1) *at / to / how / in* skateboard. I'm going to demonstrate what to do and Lily's going to be the instructor because she's good 2) *for / in / to / at* explaining things clearly. She'll tell everyone how to stand on the board and how to move your body to make the board go where you want.
Paul

Hey Paul
There's something we forgot to think about. How will we decide who learns best? I suggest that 10) *by / on / at / in* the end of the week the learners take a test. We'll give one point for each movement. Anyone who can't stand on the board will fail the test. What do you think?
Lily

2 Read all the emails. Choose the correct answer (1–10).

Hi Paul!
Yes, that does sound fun. I wish I was at your school. I'd like to see how it works. I guess the students will learn more quickly 3) *to / about / than / as* the teachers. In fact, I think it 4) *will / does / shouldn't / won't* be very hard for teachers to learn to skateboard. You can skateboard very 5) *hard / good / well / better* so you make it look as easy 6) *as / for / than / to* riding a bike. I can imagine you skating down the corridors!
Jess

VOCABULARY
School and education

1 Find the odd word out in each group.

1 fail	pass	take	<u>teach</u>
2 examiner	learner	lesson	teacher
3 classroom	timetable	library	corridor
4 test	exam	lesson	grade
5 exam	learn	revise	teach
6 practise	teacher	revise	study
7 skill	miss	fail	pass
8 practise	revise	curriculum	study

2 Choose the correct words.

1 Check your *curriculum/timetable* to see what lessons you have each week and what time your lessons are each day.

2 We have *a break/an exam* between lessons in the morning.

3 One important *grade/rule* in our school is that you mustn't run in the *corridor/exam*.

4 In an oral test, the *examiner/learner* asks you questions and gives you a grade.

5 I'll get my exam results next week. I hope I *pass/take* them.

6 Did you *fail/revise* for the test today?

3 Complete the text with these words.

~~curriculum~~   fail   grades   learn   pass
practise   revise   teach   tests   timetable

The 1) *curriculum* sets out all the subjects you have to 2) _____ at school. You take exams at the end of the year. It's important to 3) _____ the exams. For the last few weeks before the exams, the 4) _____ changes. The teachers don't 5) _____ any new material, you just 6) _____ everything you learnt in the year. You do 7) _____ in school to prepare for the exams and to see whether you are likely to get good 8) _____. It's important to 9) _____ for the exams, because you don't want to 10) _____ them.

4 Complete the notice. Use one word in each space.

Plan for success

Do you want to 1) _____*pass*_____ your exams?
Follow these 2) _____ and you will get good 3) _____ .
It's important to 4) _____ , so make time to study every day.
Make a 5) _____ for your revision, with time for each subject.
Don't work for a long time without taking a 6) _____ . Little and often is the best way to learn.

5 Find and write ten adverbs.

c	l	e	a	r	l	y	r	e
h	a	s	l	o	x	r	e	a
h	a	r	d	i	s	y	g	s
a	q	u	e	l	o	y	u	i
p	f	t	o	f	w	e	l	l
p	f	a	s	t	u	k	a	y
i	c	m	n	o	p	l	r	p
l	s	l	o	w	l	y	l	y
y	q	u	i	c	k	l	y	y

1 _____*clearly*_____   2 _____
3 _____   4 _____
5 _____   6 _____
7 _____   8 _____
9 _____   10 _____

6 Choose the correct words.

1 Read the instructions *careful/carefully* because it's *easy/easily* to make a mistake.

2 It's a *good/well* idea to practise *regular/regularly*.

3 Harry is able to learn lessons *quick/quickly* and explain them *clear/clearly*.

4 Holly will be *happy/happily* to help you, if you ask her *nice/nicely*.

5 Aiden left early, but he walks very *slow/slowly*, so I'll *easy/easily* catch up with him.

6 The key to doing *good/well* in your exam is *careful/carefully* planning.

7 Jack's writing is *clear/clearly* and *easy/easily* to read.

8 Jessica smiled *happy/happily* when she heard that her grades were *good/well*.

7 Complete the text with the correct form of these adjectives.

~~clear~~   easy   fast   good (x2)   hard (x2)
quick   regular (x2)

💬 View previous comments   Cancel   Share   Post

I'm learning to play the guitar. Three months ago, I bought a book called *How to play the guitar*. The pages are set out very 1) *clearly* and the instructions are 2) _____ to follow. At first I made 3) _____ progress. The book says 4) _____ practice is important and I played every day. So, in the beginning, I was working 5) _____ and I was learning 6) _____. However, I 7) _____ got bored with the songs in the book. It's 8) _____ to play songs you don't really like, so I stopped practising 9) _____. Then I joined a band. I wanted to play 10) _____ because the other musicians were brilliant.

8 Read Suzy's advice and choose the best answer, A, B or C, for each space.

Dear Suzy

Dear Suzy,

Can you help me?

I'm trying to train my dog, but it isn't 1) *easy* to explain things to a dog. The problem is, I don't think my dog is very 2) _____. It doesn't learn 3) _____!

Holly

Suzy Says
Hi Holly,
You have to practise 4) _____. Be 5) _____ to plan a training lesson every day. It's a 6) _____ idea to keep the lessons short, so the dog doesn't get bored. Try to be 7) _____ and remember to speak 8) _____ to the dog.

1 **A** easily   **B** easy   **C** hard
2 **A** clever   **B** cleverly   **C** fast
3 **A** quick   **B** quickly   **C** hard
4 **A** regular   **B** well   **C** regularly
5 **A** careful   **B** carefully   **C** clear
6 **A** well   **B** hard   **C** good
7 **A** quick   **B** quickly   **C** hard
8 **A** soft   **B** quiet   **C** quietly

GRAMMAR
Making comparisons

1 Complete the table with the comparatives of these adjectives.

bad	1)	*worse*
big	2)	
clever	3)	
difficult	4)	
easy	5)	
fast	6)	
fit	7)	
good	8)	
nervous	9)	
nice	10)	
noisy	11)	
fun	12)	

2 Complete the questions with the correct form of these adjectives.

clear   easy   far   ~~fast~~   good
hard   high   loud

Can you

1 … write as ___*fast*___ as you can speak?
2 … play the piano as _____ as you can sing?
3 … hit the ball as _____ as you can kick it?
4 … remember numbers as _____ as you can remember words?
5 … shout as _____ as you can whistle?
6 … swim as _____ as you can walk?
7 … jump as _____ as you can climb?
8 … see as _____ at night as you can see in the daytime?

3 Write comparative sentences.

1 library / gym (quiet)
   The library is quieter than the gym.
   The gym isn't as quiet as the library.

2 riding a bike / running (fast)

3 calling on the phone / texting (expensive)

4 reading / writing (easy)

5 school hall / classroom (big)

6 playing the game / winning (important)

7 rock climbing / ice skating (dangerous)

8 dancing / scuba diving (safe)

9 revising regularly / revising for a long time (good)

4 Write sentences. Use *too* or *not enough*.

1 We're going to be late. You / walk / quick
   You aren't walking quickly enough.

2 Your work is very bad. You / try / hard

3 I can't reach the top shelf. I / be tall

4 I can't carry this bag. It / be heavy

5 She won't help at all. She / be lazy

6 Your playing won't improve because you / practise

7 I can't reach the top shelf. It / be high

8 I can't carry this bag. I / be strong

9 Be quiet. You / speak / loud

10 Hurry up. You / walk / slow

5 Complete the sentences with a comparative form of these words.

big   dangerous   ~~noisy~~   quiet
safe   small

1 We can't revise at home, because it's *too noisy*.

2 It's not _____ to revise at home.

3 We can't cycle to school because the road is _____.

4 It's not _____ to cycle to school.

5 The TV won't fit in here. The cupboard is _____.

6 It's not _____.

LISTENING

1 Before you listen to Mia and Lucas, look at the poster. Choose what you think they will talk about.

1 Their school timetable
2 Holiday activities for teenagers
3 Their family holiday

What are you doing in the holidays?

**Ten days of different activities.
For the full programme, check out our website.**

2 🔊 4.1 Listen to Mia and Lucas and choose the correct answer, A, B or C.

1 How many days does the holiday programme last?
   A one day
   B one week
   C ten days

2 When does each day start?
   A eight thirty
   B seven o'clock
   C ten o'clock

3 What activities can students do in the mornings?
   A acting
   B sports
   C chess

4 What activity does Lucas want to do?
   A theatre
   B skateboarding
   C music

5 What does Lucas think about having language lessons?
   A It's more interesting than going to school.
   B It's not as relaxing as watching films.
   C It sounds better than staying at home.

GRAMMAR
Present continuous and present simple for future use and *shall*

1 Write sentences. Use the present continuous.

1 I / come / to see you tomorrow
   I'm coming to see you tomorrow.

2 We / take / our maths exam next week

3 We / have / pizza for lunch on Saturday

4 Isla and Max / watch / the film with us tonight / ?

5 You / not learn / to swim next term

6 Jacob / play / chess tomorrow

2 Choose the correct words.

1 My Dad *drives/is driving* me to school tomorrow.
2 The bus to town *leaves/is leaving* at 4.30.
3 *I don't take/I'm not taking* the bus into town this afternoon.
4 *Shall we/Do we* watch a DVD tonight?
5 *They show/They're showing* a new film at the cinema next Saturday.
6 School *starts/is starting* at 8.30 every day next year.
7 *Do I/Shall I* help you with your homework?
8 *We have/We're having* a party tonight.

3 Complete the conversation with the correct form of the verbs in brackets.

Amy: Hi, Holly, I checked the timetable. The train 1) _leaves_ (leave) at half past three tomorrow.

Holly: Hi, Amy. OK, 2) _____ (I / buy) the tickets online?

Amy: Yes, that's a good idea. I'll tell Jon we 3) _____ (meet) at the station at three o'clock because he's always late.

Amy: My dad 4) _____ (drive) me to the station. 5) _____ (we / pick) you up?

Holly: Great! Thank you! What time 6) _____ (you / come) to my house?

Amy: At quarter to three. The train takes half an hour, so we 7) _____ (get) to town around four o'clock.

Holly: And the film 8) _____ (start) at four thirty. Perfect!

SPEAKING SKILLS

1 **Put the words in the correct order to make sentences.**

1 to / I / skateboarding / do / . / prefer /
I prefer to do skateboarding.

2 think / I / it's / . / staying / better / at / home / than

3 rather / team / play / game / a / . / I'd

4 more / . / It's / lessons / than / relaxing / having

2 **Are the sentences for describing preferences (D) or giving reasons (G).**

1 I like staying in bed until ten o'clock when there's no school. *D*

2 I think team games are more fun than individual sports. ____

3 The screen is bigger and the sound is louder. ____

4 I'd rather watch a film at the cinema. ____

5 I prefer not to have lessons in the evening. ____

6 It's easier to learn in the morning. ____

7 I prefer football to swimming. ____

8 I'd rather not get up early when I'm on holiday. ____

WRITING

1 **Match the headings (1–5) with the different parts of an email (a–e).**

1 Starting *d*

2 Talking about plans ____

3 Giving an explanation ____

4 Making a suggestion ____

5 Ending ____

a Why don't you come with us? And would you like to bring your dog?

b See you soon. Jess.

c We're leaving from my house at 9.30 because it will take an hour to get there.

d Hi Sam,

e I'm going to the beach for my birthday on Saturday. Annie and Rick are coming too.

2 **Put the sentences of Sam's email reply in the correct order (1–5).**

a Why don't we have a picnic on the beach? ____

b I'll set my alarm so I'm not late! ____

c That's a great idea! I'd love to come. ____

d Bye for now, Sam ____

e Dear Jess, *1*

3 **Read the text message from Josh and write an email reply. Say you would like to go and ask for more information. Write 60–80 words.**

Hey
Trip to the zoo tomorrow. Dad taking sister and me. Want to come? Leave 9 am. back around 6.30.
Josh

Questions you might ask:

• How are you travelling (car, train)?

• What do I need to bring (food for lunch, money for travel or lunch)?

• Where are we going to meet? (home, station, Josh's house)?

Revision Units 3 – 4

VOCABULARY

1 Complete the sentences with one or two words in each space. The first letter has been given.

1 It's very hot here, so we need a _ir conditioning_ .

2 My hair's wet. Can I borrow your h_____?

3 This is a silk shirt, so make sure the i_____ isn't too hot.

4 Please put the dirty plates in the d_____.

5 I need to connect the speakers to the electricity supply, but there isn't a p_____.

6 All your dirty clothes are in the w_____.

7 You won't hear the music if I use my h_____.

8 I use h_____ because I don't want my hair to be curly.

9 I'll heat your dinner in the m_____.

10 The butter is in the f_____.

2 Complete the sentences with a suitable phrasal verb.

1 You left your bedroom light on.
You forgot to _switch off_ your bedroom light.

2 Your dirty clothes are on the floor.
I want you to _____ your dirty clothes.

3 I need to connect the iron to the electricity supply.
I need to _____ the iron.

4 I want to watch a TV programme.
Please _____ the TV.

5 I can't hear the radio.
Please _____ the radio.

6 The music is too loud.
Please _____ the music.

3 Complete the crossword.

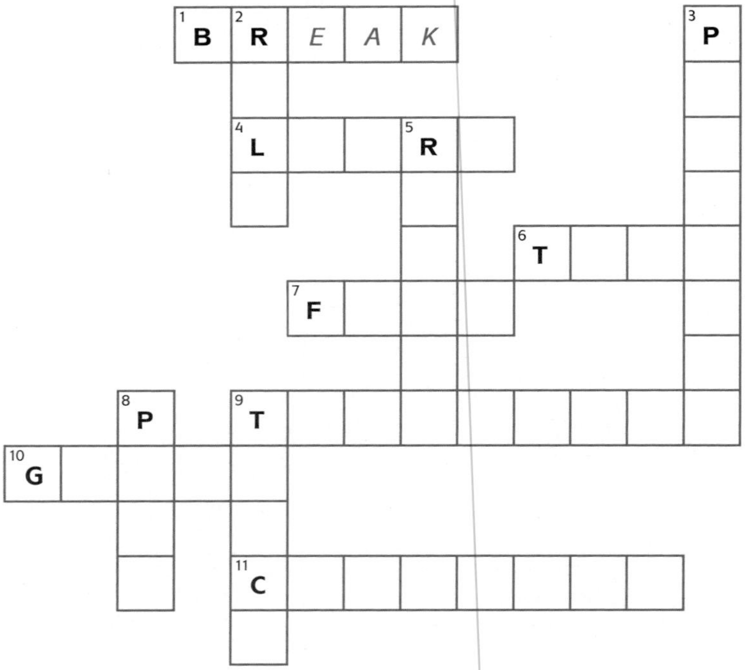

	¹B	²R	E	A	K				³P

(crossword grid)

1 B R E A K 3 P
4 L   5 R
6 T
7 F
8 P 9 T
10 G
11 C

Across

1 A time between lessons
4 To have lessons
6 A list of questions that checks how much students know
7 To be unsuccessful in an exam
9 A list of lessons and times for each day of the week
10 The mark that a teacher gives for school work
11 A long narrow area in a building, with rooms on each side

Down

2 Something you must or mustn't do
3 To do exercises
5 To study for a test or an exam
8 To be successful in an exam
9 To give lessons to

GRAMMAR

1 Complete the text with the correct forms of *going to* or *will* and the verbs in brackets.

💬 View previous comments   Cancel · Share Post

My brother, my sister and I are all 1) *going to learn* (learn) some new skills this year.
Oliver 2) _____ (learn) to play the drums. He says he 3) _____ (work) very hard. He's made a timetable and he 4) _____ (practise) regularly.
Sophie wants to learn to dance. Her friend from Hawaii says she 5) _____ (teach) her hula dancing. They 6) _____ (not do) anything else, they 7) _____ (spend) all their time dancing!
I 8) _____ (study) Japanese. I know I 9) _____ (find) it hard to learn because I'm not good at languages. I know learning Japanese 10) _____ (not be) easy because the alphabet is so different. It will take a long time, but I 11) _____ (not give up).

Write a comment   Support

2 Complete the sentences with these words.

anyone ~~anything~~ everyone everything
no one nothing someone something

1 You aren't allowed to take ____*anything*____ into the exam room to help you, no dictionaries, calculators or mobile phones.
2 You must leave _____ on the table outside the exam room – all your bags, phones and dictionaries.
3 Is there _____ in the office?
4 I hope that _____ will answer the phone.
5 Make sure that there's _____ in your bag or your pockets.
6 There's _____ here. The room is empty.
7 You'll have to wait a long time, so take _____ to read.
8 Is _____ here now or are we still waiting for some more people?

3 Write comparative sentences.

1 Heating food in an oven / not / fast / heating food in a microwave
Heating food in an oven isn't as fast as heating food in a microwave.
2 Checking words in a printed dictionary / not / quick / checking words online
3 Is watching films on 3D TV / good / watching films on ordinary TV / ?
4 My new headphones / not / comfortable / my old ones
5 The robot vacuum cleaner / quiet / the old vacuum cleaner
6 A mobile phone / not / expensive / a computer

4 Write sentences with *too* or *enough*.

1 The iron / be hot. It burned my shirt.
The iron was too hot. It burned my shirt.
2 Put the pizza in the microwave. It / not be warm
3 Turn the music down. It / be loud
4 The food isn't fresh. The fridge / not be cold
5 I don't want to watch the film. It / not be interesting
6 We can't buy a 3D TV because it / be expensive

5 Choose the correct verbs.

Max: 1) *I visit/I'm visiting* the technology fair at the weekend. What 2) *do you do/are you doing*?
Lucy: 3) *I don't do/I'm not doing* anything special.
Max: Do you want to come with me? 4) *Shall/Will* I get another ticket?
Lucy: OK, yes, I'd like to come. What time?
Max: The exhibition 5) *opens/is opening* at nine o'clock, but 6) *I don't plan/I'm not planning* to get there early. 7) *I leave/I'm leaving* home at 9.30. 8) *I cycle/I'm cycling*, so it will take me about half an hour.
Lucy: OK, let's meet there, around ten o'clock.
Max: I want to see the food technology show. 9) *They explain/They're explaining* how listening to different sounds changes the way food tastes. 10) *It starts/It's starting* at eleven o'clock.
Lucy: OK, see you on Saturday.

READING

1 Quickly read what the four people say. What are they talking about?

1 winning sports events
2 reasons for keeping fit
3 taking up new sports

Sam

I haven't done any sport since I started revising for my exams. I don't want to do an indoor sport, because I haven't been out for ages. I've never learned to ride a bike and I don't like swimming. Oh, and I haven't got a lot of money.

I already go running and I enjoy it, but I'm bored with always running in the same place. I want to take up a new sport, something challenging or something I haven't tried yet.

Ava

Noah

I've already got a bike, but I've never thought of cycling as a sport. I use it to go to school and into town. I'd really like to compete against other people and see how fast I can go.

I'm quite fit, but I'd like to do a real sport and learn some new skills. I don't have a lot of time, so I can only train once a week.

Harry

2 Read the notices (A–F). Decide which sport is the best one for each person.

1 Sam   _E_   3 Noah   _____
2 Ava   _____   4 Harry   _____

A
Climbing
If you've never done any climbing, this is the best way to start. Experience the challenge of climbing in the best conditions at our indoor climbing wall. Our qualified trainers are available every Saturday morning.

B
Sprint cycling
You've always thought of your bike as a means of transport, but it can also be the key to an exciting sport. We'll teach you new skills and train you for racing on our special track. Cycling has just got serious.

C
Tennis
Are you serious about tennis? Do you want to win? Professional coaches can help you improve your game. We train on indoor courts, so rain never stops play. Your own racket and tennis shoes required.

D
Free running
Have you heard of free running? It's a real sport that can keep you fit, but it's much more fun than running around a track. We climb buildings and jump over walls. Take up the challenge! Beginners' classes on Monday, Wednesday and Friday.

E
Kiteboarding club
Do you want to get outside and do something exciting? Have you ever tried kiteboarding? Don't worry about the weather, good or bad we're on the beach every day having fun. We supply all the equipment you need.

F
Free swimming
Are you a strong swimmer? Are you fed up with swimming pool lanes? Every Wednesday and Saturday we go free swimming in local rivers and lakes. You'll get fit and make friends and enjoy being outdoors in the natural environment.

VOCABULARY
Sport

1 Complete the crossword.

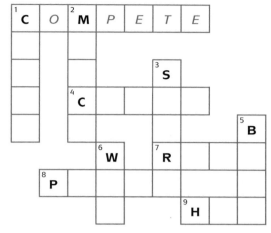

| | | | | | | |
|C|O|M|P|E|T|E|

Crossword grid with:
1. C O M P E T E (across)
2. M (down)
3. S (down)
4. C (across)
5. B (down)
6. W (down)
7. R (across)
8. P (across)
9. H (across)

Across

1 Try to win against
4 Person who trains the team
7 Competition where you try to go faster than others
8 What the winner gets
9 Move the racket against

Down

1 Place to play tennis
2 Sports event between two people or teams
3 .... a goal
5 Get more points than your opponent
6 Be the best in the game

2 Match the verbs (1–6) with the nouns (a–f).

1 beat	a a match
2 hit	b a goal
3 play	c an opponent
4 run	d a prize
5 score	e a ball
6 win	f a race

3 Complete the sentences with these words.

changing rooms   kick   ~~locker~~   prize
race   track   train

1 Everyone has a ___locker___ in the .... where they keep their sports clothes and equipment.
2 The running club meets at the .... on Wednesday afternoon.
3 Did Evie run in the 400 metre .... today?
4 To score a goal in football, you .... the ball into the net.
5 Jacob won the running competition, so he got the ....
6 The new coach is helping us .... for the competition.

4 Choose the correct words.

Max: What sports do you do at school, Isla?

Isla: I play tennis in the summer. I'm getting better, especially now that I've got a new 1) *board/racket*. We play on the 2) *court/track* at the sports centre and the coach is helping us to 3) *score/train*.

Max: How often do you play?

Isla: Every Friday. And next week I'm playing a 4) *match/race* against Holly. She 5) *beat/won* me last time we played because she 6) *hits/kicks* the ball really hard. I don't think I'll win a 7) *locker/prize*, but I'll enjoy playing. What about you?

Max: I'm doing sprint cycling. I've just got a new bike and a 8) *helmet/wetsuit*.

5 Complete the sentences with the correct sport words. The first letter has been given.

1 You need a h _e l m e t_ for sprint cycling.
2 The kiteboarding club will lend you a w............... .
3 Evie bought a new r............... to play tennis.
4 Boxers wear special g............... .
5 You can hire a b............... to go surfing.
6 Don't forget your g............... for swimming.

6 Choose the correct answer, A, B, C or D.

1 Every year, schools in our town .... against each other in sports events.
A race   B score
C compete   D beat

2 Let's play tennis this afternoon. I'll meet you at the tennis ....
A match   B court
C race   D prize

3 Did you watch the football .... on Saturday?
A score   B goal
C competition D match

4 Our new .... has encouraged the team to train harder this year.
A coach   B player
C train   D winner

5 Ethan didn't .... any goals today.
A win   B hit
C score   D kick

6 We have to .... this match to stay in the competition.
A beat   B compete
C win   D lose

7 Harry ran the 10 km .... in 45 minutes.
A court   B match
C track   D race

8 Do you think Isla will .... Sophie?
A win   B beat
C compete   D match

7 Find the odd one out in each group.

1	helmet	_race_	racket	wetsuit
2	coach	court	locker	track
3	goggles	racket	surfboard	wetsuit
4	changing room	compete	kick	win
5	beat	hit	lose	prize
6	gloves	practise	score	train
7	match	game	race	player
8	winner	player	score	coach

8 Complete the email with these words.

> beat   coach   compete   court   ~~matches~~
> practise   prizes   score

mailbox   Today | **Mail** | Calendar | Contacts

Reply | Reply All | Forward | Delete
From: **Jake**   Subject: **Hi**

Hi Mum
I'm really enjoying summer camp. You won't believe it, but I'm in the top tennis group! We play
1) _matches_ on the tennis 2) ...., but we 3) .... by hitting the ball against the wall. Our 4) .... says it's a good way to train. It's true that our group is the best. We 5) .... the other groups and we win a lot of the 6) .... But I think it's more fun to 7) .... against my friends and to see who can 8) .... more points.
Two more weeks to enjoy and then back to school!
Love
Jake

GRAMMAR
Present perfect simple

1 Write sentences. Use the present perfect form of the verbs.

1 I / play / in a lot of football matches this term
I've played in a lot of football matches this term.

2 Our team / not win / any matches this year

3 I not / try / mud running, but I'd like to

4 You look hot. You / go / running / ?

5 You / put / your clothes in your locker / ?

6 Jacob / start / learning kickboxing with the new coach

7 The school / buy / some new footballs

8 They / stop / climbing because the wall isn't safe

2 Rewrite the sentences with the adverbs in brackets in the correct place.

1 The match has started. (just)
   The match has just started.

2 Sam has swum six lengths. (already)

3 Grace hasn't changed into her sports clothes. (yet)

4 Has the match started? (already)

5 Alfie has won the prize! (just)

6 The match hasn't finished. (yet).

7 We've joined the water polo team. (already)

8 They have found the key to the changing room. (just)

9 We haven't seen the new swimming pool. (yet)

10 You can't leave, our team is winning! (yet)

3 Look at the chart and write sentences. Use the present perfect form and *already/yet* where appropriate.

	Jack	Amelia
decide to get fit	✓	✓
buy tennis rackets	✓	✓
join a club	✗	✗
have a tennis lesson	✗	✓
win a match	✓	✗

1 Jack and Amelia __*have decided to get fit*__ .
2 They _____ .
3 They _____ .
4 Jack _____ .
5 Amelia _____ .
6 Jack _____ ,
   but Amelia _____ .

4 Complete the blog with the present perfect form of the verbs in brackets.

💬 View previous comments   Cancel   Share   Post

There are lots of new sports to try at the sports centre. They 1) *have just employed* (just / employ) some new coaches for kickboxing, tennis, water polo and sprint cycling. I'm good at swimming, so I 2) _____ (already / join) the water polo team, but we 3) _____ (not have / our first training session / yet). I'm interested in the sprint cycling, but I 4) _____ (not get / a bike / yet). The kickboxing coach 5) _____ (just / put up) the timetable and I 6) _____ (already / pay) for the first lesson.

Write a comment   Support

LISTENING

1 🔊 5.1 Listen to Max and Grace talk about a new club. Are the sentences (1–6) true (T) or false (F)?

1 About 50 people came to the breakdancing demonstration. __T__

2 Getting a text message encouraged people to come to the demonstration. _____

3 More people have watched breakdancing than tried it. _____

4 The demonstration was popular, but only a few people want to learn how to breakdance. _____

5 They've already chosen the music for the first lesson. _____

6 Max and Grace agree on the style of music. _____

GRAMMAR
Past simple and present perfect simple

1 Choose the correct form of the verbs.

1 Yesterday's match _was_/has been very exciting.
2 I _didn't run_/hadn't run a race this afternoon.
3 I _cycled_/have cycled to school today.
4 _Did the race finish?_/Has the race finished?
5 How many people _took_/have taken part in the New York Marathon this year?
6 Our football team _trained_/has trained really hard this year, so I hope they win.
7 We _didn't play_/haven't played tennis for weeks!
8 _We just won_/We've just won the competition!
9 Our training session _didn't start_/hasn't started yet because the coach is late.
10 Two cyclists _fell off_/has fallen off their bikes during the final lap of the race.

2 Write the responses in the conversation.

Olivia: Hey, you two. Look at all the new sports we can do at the sports centre now.

Lucy: 1) You / try sprint cycling / ?
Have you tried sprint cycling?

Olivia: No, I haven't. I haven't got a bike. What about you?

Lucy: 2) I / try / sprint cycling / last week, but I / not like / it

_____

Olivia: What about you, Dan?

Dan: 3) I / join / the water polo team

_____

Olivia: Is it fun?

Dan: 4) We / have / a training session yesterday, but we / not play / a match yet

_____

Lucy: Sounds great. Maybe we should join, too.

Olivia: 5) I never / play / water polo

_____

Dan: Well, why don't you both come? We've got another training session this afternoon.

Lucy: 6) I not / finish / last week's homework yet

_____

Olivia: I haven't got any homework. I'll come!

3 Complete the sentences with the correct form of these verbs and the words in brackets.

> buy   find   have   run   see   start
> ~~swim~~   try   win

1 We often swim in the pool, but we _'ve never swum_ (never) in the river before.
2 I don't think Thomas will complete the course, he _____ (never) a marathon before.
3 Our school _____ two prizes in the sports competition last week.
4 I _____ (just) some goggles, because I'm taking up synchronised swimming.
5 William lost his racket yesterday. _____ (he) it yet?
6 The match _____ at three o'clock.
7 Congratulations! This is the first time I _____ (ever) you win a race!
8 _____ (you ever) kickboxing?
9 I _____ my first swimming lesson yesterday.

4 Complete the email with the correct form of the verbs in brackets.

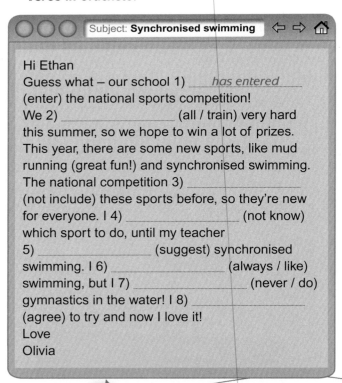

Subject: **Synchronised swimming**

Hi Ethan
Guess what – our school 1) _has entered_ (enter) the national sports competition!
We 2) _____ (all / train) very hard this summer, so we hope to win a lot of prizes.
This year, there are some new sports, like mud running (great fun!) and synchronised swimming.
The national competition 3) _____ (not include) these sports before, so they're new for everyone. I 4) _____ (not know) which sport to do, until my teacher 5) _____ (suggest) synchronised swimming. I 6) _____ (always / like) swimming, but I 7) _____ (never / do) gymnastics in the water! I 8) _____ (agree) to try and now I love it!
Love
Olivia

SPEAKING SKILLS

1 Match the questions (1–6) with the answers (a–f).

1 Who is in the photo? _c_
2 Where are they? _____
3 What are they wearing? _____
4 What are they doing? _____
5 How are they feeling? _____
6 What do you think about this activity? _____

a They're wearing helmets and lifejackets.
b It looks fun. I've never done it, but it looks exciting.
c It's a group of friends, or members of a club.
d They're at the coast because there are rocks and water.
e They're climbing the rocks.
f I think they're excited but also nervous because it's dangerous.

2 Complete the description. Use one word in each space.

"The photo 1) s _hows_ a group of friends. They 2) c_____ be members of a club. They're at the coast because the sea is in the 3) b_____ and there are rocks. I think it 4) m_____ be dangerous because they're wearing helmets and life jackets. It 5) l_____ exciting but it could be dangerous, too! "
Emily

WRITING

1 Complete the school magazine article. Use these words and phrases.

although   as soon as   because   either
except   or   ~~so that~~

How I feel about school sports
By Harry

A) When I was at school, I hated sports. No one ever wanted me to be in their football team. At first, I tried to hide in the library 1) _so that_ I didn't have to take part in the team sports. When the teacher noticed me, she suggested I try running 2) _____ it's not a team sport. I hated it. Running is really boring.

B) Then one day, I saw a notice in the library about a new sport, kickboxing at the gym. I decided to try it and 3) _____ I started, I loved it. Now, I train every day, 4) _____ at home 5) _____ at the gym. I've met a lot of people at the kickboxing club, and made a lot of new friends.

C) I still don't like team sports 6) _____ I'm stronger and more confident now. I wasn't interested in any sports 7) _____ kickboxing until I watched people climbing the wall at the gym. I've decided to try that because it looks good fun.

2 Read the article again. Match the ideas (1–3) to the paragraphs (A–C).

1 A sport that Harry wants to try. _____
2 How Harry felt about sports at school. _____
3 A sport that Harry has tried and liked. _____

3 Read the questions and make notes for you.

1 Which sports do you do at school? _____
2 How do you feel about school sports? Give reasons for your answer. _____
3 Which sports do you like? _____
   I like _____
   because I enjoy _____
4 Which sports don't you like?
   I don't like _____
   because _____
5 What are the advantages of doing sport?
   Sport helps you _____
   and _____
6 Do you do any sport outside school? Why/Why not?

4 Write an article, 'How I feel about school sports!' Use your notes and write three paragraphs. Write about 120 words.

READING

1 Choose the best caption, **A** or **B**, for each photo. Read the text opposite quickly to check your answers.

1 A I love playing cricket on the beach.
  B My Australian classmates are all very sporty.

2 A A kangaroo can be dangerous.
  B A kangaroo makes a good pet.

2 Read the text again. Are the sentences (1–10) true (T) or false (F)?

1 Joseph has lived in Australia for a long time. _F_
2 Joseph isn't going to have a pet kangaroo. ....
3 Joseph's family moved to Australia for work. ....
4 Joseph has the same interests as most people in his class. ....
5 Joseph likes the beach near his new home. ....
6 Australians enjoy sports at the beach. ....
7 Joseph would rather read than play cricket. ....
8 Joseph is going to try to find friends online. ....
9 Joseph was frightened by the kangaroo in the car park. ....
10 Nobody took any notice of the kangaroo. ....

My life down under

My family have just moved to Australia. I started at a new school last month and I'm having a hard time. I was really excited when my Dad said he had a job in Australia. I thought it would be an amazing place to live. The problem is that I haven't got anything in common with the people in my class. They're all very sporty and go to the beach every day after school. The local beach is beautiful and at home I loved swimming in the sea and sunbathing – but the Australians don't do that! The sea here is dangerous for someone like me because I can't swim very well. There are huge waves and everyone goes surfing. When they're tired of surfing they play cricket on the beach. If I liked sports, I could spend time with them, but I'm much happier sitting in a deckchair reading a book. My classmates think that's boring! I don't think I'll really make friends unless I find people with similar interests.

I've decided that the best way to get to know people is to look for friends on social networking sites. I like reading, so I might find people I can get on with if I join a book group. I'm also interested in animals, and there are some very strange animals in Australia. Yesterday there was a kangaroo in the car park! Everyone was looking at it. People were laughing and pointing at the kangaroo and it became very frightened. In the end, a policeman asked everyone to stay calm, and be quiet. He managed to catch the kangaroo and take it away. That could never happen in England! I'd like to have a kangaroo as a pet, but it's not really a good idea. An adult kangaroo is big and they are dangerous because they might kick you.

Joseph

VOCABULARY
Friendship and feelings

1 **Choose the correct phrases and phrasal verbs.**

1 I'd like to be friends, I don't want to *get to know/fall out with* you.
2 It's better to *deal with/spend time with* the problem.
3 I'm sorry you've had *a lot in common/a hard time* recently.
4 Do you *get to know/have a lot in common with* your brothers and sisters?
5 Let's *stay calm/get on with each other* and talk about it.
6 I'm going to *spend time with/deal with* my grandparents in the holidays.
7 Oscar *deals with/gets on well with* Mia.
8 How did you *get to know/have a lot in common with* each other?

2 **Put the words in the correct order to make sentences.**

1 stay / Try / calm / to / .
   Try to stay calm.
2 time / spend / my friends / I / with / like / to / .
   ....
3 in common / Jacob / a lot / and / Noah / have / .
   Jacob ....
4 Lily / Amelia / on / gets / with / .
   Lily ....
5 out / Max / with / Charlie / fell / .
   Max ....
6 at school / Chloe / know / each other / got / Jessica / to / and / .
   Chloe ....

3 **Replace the underlined phrases.**

> deal with   fall out with   get on with
> ~~get to know~~   a hard time   stay calm
> have a lot in common   spend time with

1 I'd like to <u>become friends with</u> William, he's fun.
   I'd like to get to know William, he's fun.
2 Holly is having <u>some difficult problems</u> at the moment.
   ....
3 I've got a problem at school and I don't know how to <u>find a way to stop</u> it.
   ....
4 You should <u>stop yourself getting upset or angry</u> and not shout at your brother.
   ....
5 I'd like to <u>be together with</u> you this weekend.
   ....
6 My sister is older than me and we don't <u>share the same ideas or interests</u>.
   ....
7 I didn't want to <u>argue with</u> Ed, but he was very rude.
   ....
8 Do you <u>have a good relationship with</u> your sister?
   ....

4 **Complete the text with the best answer, A, B, C or D, for each space.**

> My cousins, Sam and Eliza, live on the other side of the country, so I hardly ever see them and I didn't know them well. But during the school holidays I really 1) __*got*__ to know them. They came to stay with us and we 2) _____ a lot of time together. We discovered that we 3) _____ a lot in common. They've had a 4) _____ time recently because their father lost his job. Fortunately, our parents get on 5) _____ each other and my mother advised Uncle George how to deal 6) _____ the situation. She told him to 7) _____ calm and not fall 8) _____ with the man he worked for.

1	**A** get	**B** got	**C** had	**D** have
2	**A** stay	**B** stayed	**C** spent	**D** spend
3	**A** have	**B** hold	**C** get	**D** got
4	**A** good	**B** worse	**C** fast	**D** hard
5	**A** to	**B** with	**C** at	**D** for
6	**A** for	**B** at	**C** with	**D** about
7	**A** hold	**B** have	**C** get	**D** stay
8	**A** out	**B** in	**C** off	**D** against

5 Complete the crossword with adjectives ending in *-ed* or *-ing*.

Crossword grid:

1 Across: A M A Z I N G
3 Across: E _ _ _ _ _
4 Down: F
5 Down/Across: B
6 Across: S _ _ _ _ _ _
7 Across: A _ _ _ _ _
8 Across: E _ _ _ _ _ _ _ _ _

Across

1 It's .... what you can do when you try!
3 We're all .... about the concert!
6 The news about Oscar winning a prize was really .... I didn't know he played chess so well.
7 I'm really .... with Tom, he's upset me.
8 Holly heard what I said about her and I was really .... My face went red!

Down

2 The programme about horses was very ....
4 The horses were .... by the loud noises.
5 I don't like this game, I think it's ....

6 Choose the correct words.

1 It's *surprising*/*boring* how well Lily and Noah get on.
2 I'm *bored*/*amazed* with this game. Let's play something else.
3 There's no mobile phone signal here. It's really *annoying*/*exciting*.
4 Please don't shout in front of everyone in the café. It's very *embarrassing*/*surprising*.
5 I'm *annoyed*/*bored* that you didn't tell me you weren't coming!
6 There's no need to feel *amazed*/*embarrassed*. I understand how you feel.
7 Were you and Sophie *surprised*/*interested* to find out that you have something in common?
8 I don't want to spend time with Alfie and William. They're *amazing*/*boring*.

7 Complete the film review with one word in each space. The first letter has been given.

The boy from another world

Last night's film, *The Boy from Another World*, was very strange. At first, I thought the film was just another 1) b*oring* 'boy-meets-girl' story. A teenage girl is 2) e............... when she meets a good-looking boy. She thinks he is 3) i............... and she wants to get to know him better. She is 4) s............... to discover that he isn't an ordinary teenager like everyone else. He comes from another planet and he has 5) a............... powers.
He understands people's thoughts and he is often 6) a............... with them. When he gets angry, he does some terrible and 7) f............... things.
I have to say that I enjoyed the film. I'm 8) e............... to admit it, but at the end, when the boy went home to his own world, I cried.

GRAMMAR
Talking about ability and possibility

1 Look at the information about Charlotte's phone and Will's e-reader on page 41. Complete the sentences. Use *can* or *can't* and the verbs from the lists.

1 Charlotte ...*can make*... calls with her phone.
2 She .... text messages.
3 Charlotte .... photos.
4 She .... connect to the Internet.
5 Will .... books on his e-reader.
6 He .... to stories.
7 Will .... calls.
8 He .... text messages.

Charlotte's phone
✓ make calls
✓ send text messages
✗ take photos
✗ connect to the Internet

Will's e-reader
✓ read books
✓ listen to stories
✗ make calls
✗ send text messages

Chapter 1

Holding an ebook reader and reading an electronic book

Why should you buy an eBook reader? Instead of going to a bookstore to make a purchase or ordering a book online and waiting for it to arrive, you can purchase and download an eBook anytime, from any location with a Wi-Fi

2 Choose the correct words.

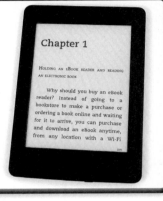

Training your dog

Do
■ keep your dog on a lead at first because it 1) *couldn't / might not* come when you call it.
■ give clear instructions. Then your dog 2) *will be able to / could* understand what you want.
■ keep training sessions short because your dog 3) *could / will be able to* become tired. A tired dog 4) *couldn't / won't be able to* concentrate.

Don't
■ let your dog take control, it 5) *could / will be able to* become dangerous.
■ encourage small children to play with your dog, it 6) *can / might* bite them and you 7) *will be able to / could* get into trouble.
■ shout at your dog. You 8) *might / will be able to* frighten it. When your dog doesn't do what you tell it, it 9) *might not / couldn't* understand what you want.

3 Complete the conversation with the best answer, A, B, C or D, for each space.

Daniel: What animals 1) *will we be able to* see at the zoo tomorrow?

Mum: We 2) _____ see lots of animals, but we'll have to choose because the zoo is very big and we 3) _____ to see everything.

Daniel: I want to see the monkeys, but they're very clever and I think they 4) _____ get out of their cages.

Mum: Don't worry. There are two doors to the cages, so that the keepers 5) _____ go inside to feed the monkeys. They lock the outside door so that the monkeys 6) _____ escape.

1 (A) will we be able to   **B** could we
   C might we   **D** can't we
2 **A** can't   **B** will be able to
   C couldn't   **D** might not
3 **A** could   **B** will be able to
   C couldn't   **D** won't be able to
4 **A** won't be able to   **B** can't
   C might   **D** couldn't
5 **A** will be able to   **B** might
   C can't   **D** can
6 **A** couldn't   **B** can't
   C might   **D** might not

4 Complete the notice with *can/can't* or *will/won't be able to*.

Can you swim?

Yes: Take a life-saving certificate. Become a lifeguard. Get a holiday job at the pool. Have fun and earn money.

No: Take a beginner's course. Learn to swim in three weeks. Have fun playing water sports and games.

You 1) *can* already swim. You 2) _____ take our advanced course. Get a life-saving certificate and qualify as a lifeguard. After that you 3) _____ get a summer job at the swimming pool. Then you 4) _____ have fun and earn money at the same time.

   You 5) _____ swim. Take our beginner's course and you 6) _____ learn to swim in three weeks. You 7) _____ get a job at the pool, but you 8) _____ have fun playing water sports and games.

LISTENING

1 🔊 **6.1 Listen to Lucy and her dad talking. Choose what Lucy is doing.**

1 Arguing
2 Finding out information
3 Asking for advice

2 🔊 **6.2 Listen again and choose the correct answer, A, B or C.**

1 What does Lucy say about Ellie?
  A She's embarrassed.
  B She's unkind.
  C She's funny.

2 How does Lucy feel when she's with Ellie?
  A She's nervous.
  B She's bored.
  C She's jealous.

3 What happens when Lucy arranges to meet Ellie?
  A Ellie comes late.
  B Ellie never comes.
  C Ellie calls to say she isn't coming.

4 Why does Lucy want to spend time with Ellie?
  A She gets on well with Ellie.
  B Ellie doesn't have any other friends.
  C Ellie is friends with everyone.

5 What does Lucy's dad suggest Lucy should ask Ellie?
  A If she's had a hard time.
  B Why she's friendly.
  C If Lucy has annoyed her.

6 What advice does Lucy's dad give her?
  A To wait for Ellie.
  B To spend time with other people.
  C To let the problem go away.

GRAMMAR
Zero conditional, first conditional and *unless*

1 Match (1–6) with (A–F) to make sentences.

1 If you have something in common with someone, _E_
2 If she apologises to me, _____
3 If you don't want to spend time with me, _____
4 If you can't deal with a problem, _____
5 If you stay calm, _____
6 If you want to get to know Ryan, _____

A please tell me.
B I'll introduce you.
C you'll be able to explain the problem.
D we won't fall out.
E you usually get on with them.
F ask a friend to help you.

2 Rewrite the sentences using *unless*.

1 Don't tell James if you don't want everyone to know.
   Don't tell James unless you want everyone to know.

2 Don't wait for them if they don't call you.
   _____

3 Don't come to the cinema if you don't want to see the film.
   _____

4 Let's stop and have a coffee if you aren't too busy.
   _____

5 Let's watch the documentary if you haven't already seen it.
   _____

6 We could eat later if you aren't too hungry.
   _____

3 Choose the correct words.

1 If you *want*/will want to take a photo, *you press*/you'll press this button.
2 *I send*/I'll send you an invitation if you *give*/will give me your mobile number.
3 My dog *never comes*/will never come unless *I give*/I'll give it a biscuit.
4 Your mother *is*/will be worried about you if you *don't call*/won't call her.
5 If Lily *concentrates*/will concentrate, *she always wins*/she'll always win the game.
6 If you *don't*/won't listen, you *don't*/won't know what to do.
7 You *don't*/won't get to know them unless you *talk*/will talk to them.

4 Complete the conversation with the correct form of the verbs in brackets.

Lucas

Hi Dan. Listen, I'm on my way, but I'm late. If I 1) _____miss_____ (miss) the bus, I 2) _____ (let) you know.

Dan

OK. I 3) _____ (not buy) the train tickets unless I 4) _____ (know) you're coming. Send me a text if you 5) _____ (catch) the bus.

Lucas

If I 6) _____ (be) late, please 7) _____ (tell) Dylan I'm sorry.

Dan

OK, I'm sure he 8) _____ (understand) the situation if I 9) _____ (explain) it to him.

SPEAKING SKILLS

1 Complete the phrases for apologising and responding.

1 I'm really _sorry_ . I lost the bag you lent me.
2 That's _____ . I needed a new one.
3 I tripped over your cat. I hope it isn't hurt. It was an _____ .
4 Never _____ , I'm sure the cat's fine.
5 I didn't _____ to upset you.
6 I'll be more careful in future, so it won't _____ again.

2 Put the sentences of the conversation in the correct order.

a Mum, I'm really sorry. I've broken your favourite vase. __1__

b It was an accident. It fell out of the cupboard when I was getting a mug. _____

c Well, I didn't mean to, it was next to the mug and I knocked it on the floor. _____

d Oh no! How did you do that? _____

e Oh well, never mind. You can buy me a new vase for my birthday. _____

f I don't understand. Why did you move the vase? _____

WRITING

1 Complete the email with these phrases.

by mistake   straight away   ~~up to you~~
whatever you want   you prefer

Hi Natalie,

I hope you enjoyed your holiday at the safari park. I'm looking forward to seeing the photos you took with my camera. Did you find it easy to use? You can upload the photos to our social networking site or you can put them on your computer, it's 1) _up to you_ .

I'd like to have the camera back now, because it's three weeks since you borrowed it. I think my brother may have sent you a message 2) _____ , saying you can keep it until we go back to school. In fact, I need it for tomorrow, because I'm going to Chloe's birthday party. I can come and pick it up 3) _____ or you could bring it round this afternoon, if 4) _____ . Let me know what's best for you, and I'll do 5) _____ .

Your friend,
Amy

2 Read the email again. What does Amy want Natalie to do?

1 take a photo with her camera
2 look after her camera
3 return her camera
4 pick up her camera

3 Which of these things should Natalie say to Amy in her reply?

1 Say how you will show her the photos.
2 Tell her about your journey home.
3 Thank her for lending you her camera.
4 Thank her for asking about your holiday.
5 Describe all the things you took on holiday with you.
6 Say when you will return the camera.

4 Write Natalie's email reply to Amy. Write 35–45 words. Thank her for asking about your holiday and for lending you her camera. Say how you will show her photos and when you will return the camera.

Revision Units 5 – 6

VOCABULARY

1 Find and write the sports words. There are four things to wear, two things to use and two places to do sports.

g	o	g	g	l	e	s	r	r
c	g	l	o	b	r	b	a	a
o	l	o	g	a	d	o	c	c
u	u	v	l	t	r	a	c	k
r	v	e	s	o	e	r	s	e
t	s	s	g	a	m	d	b	t
h	h	e	l	m	e	t	a	t
w	e	t	s	u	i	t	c	w
w	o	u	r	t	r	a	k	c

Things to wear
1 _____goggles_____
2 _____
3 _____
4 _____

Things to use
1 _____
2 _____

Places to do sports
1 _____
2 _____

2 Complete the sentences with these words.

> beats ~~hits~~ kicks match prizes races racket scores wins

Roger is a great tennis player. He 1) _____hits_____ the ball very hard with his 2) _____. He usually 3) _____ his opponent.

Ryan is a brilliant footballer. He 4) _____ a lot of goals. When he plays a 5) _____, he often 6) _____ the ball into the net.

Usain is a fantastic athlete. He 7) _____ a lot of 8) _____ because he runs 9) _____ very fast.

3 Choose the correct words.

Ask Aunt Lucy

Dear Aunt Lucy
I'm 1) _having_/spending/being a hard time at school. It's difficult to 2) do/get/stay calm and concentrate in class because I don't know how to 3) solve/sort/deal with the problem. Some new boys joined our class and at first it was easy to 4) fall/get/deal on with them. Now that I've 5) got/had/come to know them better, I don't think we 6) are/know/have anything in common. They are often unkind to other people in the class. I don't want to 7) give/spend/use time with them now, but I don't want to 8) get/fall/be out with them either because I think they'll be unkind to me.
Ava

4 Complete the sentences with the correct form of the words in brackets.

1 The most ___surprising___ (surprise) thing about synchronised swimming is how hard it is!
2 I'm _____ (excite) about the final on Saturday.
3 Don't be _____ (embarrass) about not finishing the marathon. It's a very long race.
4 Cycling is an _____ (excite) sport. It's really fast.
5 I'm _____ (surprise) that you enjoy mud running. You don't like being cold and dirty.
6 Climbing may be fun to do, but it's _____ (bore) to watch!
7 Oscar was _____ (annoy) about losing the race.
8 I love kickboxing, it's an _____ (amaze) sport.

GRAMMAR

1 Complete the conversation with the present perfect form of the verbs in brackets.

George: Hi, William. 1) _Have you met_ (you / meet) Charlotte? She 2) ＿＿＿＿ (just / started) at our school. She 3) ＿＿＿＿ (already / make) a lot of friends, but I 4) ＿＿＿＿ (not introduce) her to everyone yet.

William: Hi there, Charlotte. I 5) ＿＿＿＿ (already / discover) that we've got something in common! I 6) ＿＿＿＿ (know) your cousin Sam for a long time! We 7) ＿＿＿＿ (be) friends online since last year.

Charlotte: That's great! Sam 8) ＿＿＿＿ (already / tell) me he had a friend at this school, so now I can tell him that I 9) ＿＿＿＿ (just / meet) you!

2 Complete the text with the best answer, A, B, C or D, for each space.

Summer camp	⇦ ⇨

	Cancel Share Post

George and I 1) _have been_ friends for a long time. We 2) ＿＿ at summer camp five years ago and we 3) ＿＿ on well. We 4) ＿＿ a lot of time together since we 5) ＿＿ , but last year we 6) ＿＿ each other at all. We 7) ＿＿ out and George 8) ＿＿ meeting next month. We 9) ＿＿ to go to another summer camp next year, but we 10) ＿＿ where we'll go yet.

Support

1 **A** were **(B)** have been
  C has been **D** was
2 **A** met **B** have met
  C has met **D** meet
3 **A** has got **B** have got
  C got **D** get
4 **A** have spent **B** spend
  C spent **D** has spent
5 **A** have met **B** has met
  C met **D** meet
6 **A** haven't seen **B** hasn't seen
  C don't see **D** didn't see

7 **A** hasn't fallen **B** haven't fallen
  C don't fall **D** didn't fall
8 **A** have just suggested **B** has just suggested
  C just suggested **D** just suggests
9 **A** already plan **B** has already planned
  C have already planned **D** planned
10 **A** don't decide **B** hasn't decided
  C didn't decide **D** haven't decided

3 Choose the correct words.

It's surprising what you 1) _can/could/might_ do when you try. You decide to take up running and you imagine that you 2) _can/might/will be able to_ compete in a marathon very soon. Then you start training and find you 3) _couldn't/can't/won't be able to_ run very fast and you 4) _can't/couldn't/won't be able to_ run very far. You don't give up and after a few training sessions you find that you 5) _might/could/can_ run faster than you managed at first. You think you 6) _might/can/won't be able to_ enter for a marathon next year. You hope to complete the course. You know you 7) _might/can't/won't be able to_ beat the really fast runners, but you 8) _might/can/won't be able to_ beat some people.

4 Complete the text with the correct form of the verbs in brackets.

When people 1) _watch_ (watch) sporting events on TV, they often 2) ＿＿＿＿ (start) training. If TV 3) ＿＿＿＿ (not show) women's sports or Paralympic events, people 4) ＿＿＿＿ (not know) about them. Sports 5) ＿＿＿＿ (not become) popular unless they 6) ＿＿＿＿ (be) on TV. We know that more people 7) ＿＿＿＿ (take up) cycling if a popular sports person like Bradley Wiggins 8) ＿＿＿＿ (win) the Tour de France.

That's entertainment

READING

1 Read the text quickly. What's it about?

   1 An event   **2** A special day   **3** A person

The town of Beckwood is still talking 1) *of/to/about/with* last week's musical event that surprised the whole community. It was 2) *a/an/one/the* typical Saturday morning and a lot was happening in the lively town square. The cafés were full 3) *of/about/in/off* people who were chatting and relaxing with a cup of coffee in the spring sunshine. A group of children were skateboarding around the fountain and 4) *a/any/lots/some* teenagers were chatting to friends. As usual, the streets were quite noisy 5) *because/but/so/then* nobody noticed when a young woman suddenly stood up and started to sing in the square. Then a second person started to sing and then a third. Soon more people started to sing. 6) *And/Once/When/Then*, several people began playing instruments. Was it a choir? Perhaps the school orchestra were performing a concert. Gradually the customers in the cafés stopped talking and the Saturday morning shoppers stopped buying. Soon they were all watching as the town square 7) *changed/became/prepared/turned* the stage for a flash mob.

Flash mobs started more than ten years ago. Sometimes people organise them on social networking sites or by email. The idea is that people of all ages come together and 8) *perform/entertain/review/show* an audience in a public place. In some flash mobs, the people who perform wear the same colour T-shirts or costumes. Flash mobs have 9) *happened/come/fallen/passed* in shopping centres, cafés and even on buses and trains. It's a simple idea and at the end the performers often leave as soon as they finish. The important thing is to surprise the audience and have fun.

At the end of the flash mob in Beckwood, everybody clapped. They loved it and most people wanted to watch it again. One student managed to film it on his phone. 10) 'That was *many/such/to/so* cool,' he said. 'If that happened every Saturday, I'd come and watch them.'

2 Read the text again. Choose the correct answer (1–10).

VOCABULARY
Entertainment

1 Find and write seven entertainment words.

c	e	c	r	c	c	u	e	r
h	s	r	d	r	o	w	r	i
o	r	c	h	e	s	t	r	a
i	o	o	g	x	t	c	d	i
r	o	a	c	i	u	r	a	o
a	t	e	h	t	m	e	s	g
s	m	e	e	u	e	c	a	c
a	u	d	i	e	n	c	e	i
t	r	e	e	e	c	a	t	e

1 ....*row*..........   5 ....
2 ....   6 ....
3 ....   7 ....
4 ....

2 Complete the entertainment words with *a, e, i, o* or *u*.

1 r _o_ w
2 ch.......... ....r
3 c..........st..........m..........
4 ....x..........t
5 ....d..........nc..........
6 ....rch..........str..........
7 st..........g..........

3 Write the words in Exercise 2 under the correct headings.

People	Places	Things
	row	

4 Complete the sentences with entertainment words. The first letter has been given.

1 When the show finished the a*udience*_____ stood up and left the theatre.
2 You can't sit in that r_____ . It's for the photographers.
3 Emily plays the trumpet in the school o_____ .
4 The actor came on the s_____ and started talking.
5 I'd love to sing in a c_____ , but my voice is terrible.
6 We tried to leave the concert quickly, but there were loads of people at the e_____ .
7 She didn't like her c_____ because it was too long to walk in and the fabric was heavy.
8 The r_____ of the show in the newspaper was excellent.

5 Complete the blog. Use one word in each space.

---

goodtheatreblog.com ⇦ ⇨

💬 View previous comments   Cancel   Share   Post

My local theatre is only small, but it's got
1) _*rows*_ of comfortable, red seats that are
great for relaxing and enjoying shows. Tonight the
2) _____ was full of students who came
to watch a musical by the Creative Teens Theatre
Company. A live 3) _____ played music
during the show and a 4) _____ sang an
unusual mixture of classical and pop music.
When the show finished the performers came back
on 5) _____ and continued for another half
hour. Everything was great about the show except
for the 6) _____ . The actors looked hot and
uncomfortable all night.

Write a comment   Support

6 Match the photos (A–F) with the sentences (1–6). Use the words in bold to help you.

1 They're going to **film** a documentary about the town. _E_
2 In today's programme we're **interviewing** a local pop star. _____
3 Amelia is **recording** an album of her own songs. _____
4 Everybody enjoyed **performing** in the school play. _____
5 I'm **reviewing** a film for my English homework. _____
6 The audience **clapped** for ages and finally the actors came back on stage. _____

7 Choose the correct words.

1 We're excited that they're *performing/filming* our school for the programme. We're going to be on TV!

2 Guess what? I'm *interviewing/recording* the pop group *Flippers* for the school magazine.

3 Before the show a comedian came on stage and *filmed/entertained* the audience with a few jokes.

4 If you like the cinema and writing, you could *book/review* films for a magazine.

8 Complete the text with the best answer, A, B, C or D, for each space.

This week, *Entertainment News* is 1) _reviewing_ *The Voice* – Saturday night's new talent show to find Britain's best singer.

It's a simple idea. The contestant comes onto the 2) _____ and gives a short introduction. Then the studio 3) _____ watches as he or she sings in front of four judges. The judges can't see who is 4) _____ to them because they have their backs to the singer. If they like the singer, they press a red light and their chair turns around. When this happens everybody starts 5) _____ because it means the singer is good. When more than one professional turns around, the contestant chooses which one he or she wants to work with.

The winner of the competition has the chance to 6) _____ an album. The professionals are good fun and know how to 7) _____ the audience with stories of how they became famous.

If you'd like to be in the studio audience, call now to 8) _____ tickets – they're free!

1	**A** filming	**B** recording
	C reviewing	**D** interviewing
2	**A** row	**B** stage
	C exit	**D** orchestra
3	**A** audience	**B** choir
	C orchestra	**D** costume
4	**A** performing	**B** entertaining
	C acting	**D** recording
5	**A** filming	**B** interviewing
	C booking	**D** clapping
6	**A** book	**B** perform
	C entertain	**D** record
7	**A** interview	**B** review
	C entertain	**D** perform
8	**A** record	**B** book
	C film	**D** review

GRAMMAR
Second conditional

1 Match the sentence beginnings (1–7) with the endings (A–G).

1 If I won two tickets to the festival, _F_
2 If the school had a good choir, _____
3 The theatre would lose money _____
4 If I didn't like the show, _____
5 She would learn faster _____
6 If the stage were bigger, _____
7 We wouldn't stay late at the concert _____

A I would leave early.
B if we had school the next day.
C if she practised more.
D the dancers would have more space.
E if the tickets were too cheap.
F I would ask you to come with me.
G I would sing in it.

2 Choose the correct words.

1 If I *am/were* you, I would join the school drama club.

2 If you *interview/interviewed* a famous person, what would you ask?

3 I wouldn't stay at the concert if I *don't like/didn't like* the music.

4 What would you do if you *lost/lose* your iPod?

5 If we *have/had* more music lessons at school, I'd be really happy.

6 Emily would call us if she *wanted/wants* to see us.

7 What would Liam do if he *isn't/wasn't* a pop singer?

8 I wouldn't wear that costume on stage if I *were/am* you.

3 Complete the second conditional sentences. Use the correct form of the verbs in brackets.

1 If we asked them, _would they sing_ (sing) for us?

2 I _____ (not play) the drums in here if I were you.

3 Jake and Olivia _____ (go) to the concert if they had tickets.

4 If you liked the music, _____ (dance) with me?

5 You _____ (love) this festival if you were here.

6 The audience _____ (not clap) if they weren't happy with the show.

7 _____ (you / travel) around the world if you were in a pop group?

8 If you passed the exam, you _____ (get) a place in a good music school.

4 Complete the magazine interview with the correct form of the verbs in brackets.

Every week at *Pop News* we invite our readers to ask their favourite celebrity the question 'What would you do if ...?' This week we say 'Hi' to Billy from the band IDX.

Hi, Billy, what would you do if you 1) _weren't_ **(not be) in a pop group?**

Ah, a difficult question! If I 2) _____ (not sing), I'd be really bored. Singing is my passion.

If you won the lottery, what 3) _____ **(you / buy)?**

Great question. If I 4) _____ (have) lots of money, I'd buy a big house for my family.

Billy, if you 5) _____ **(buy) a pet, what would it be?**

Well, I've already got two dogs, but if I bought another pet, it 6) _____ (be) a snake.

What would you do if you 7) _____ **(be) ill on the night of a concert?**

I'm never ill, but if I was really bad, I 8) _____ (call) the doctor.

And finally, you hate flying, Billy. What would you do if the band 9) _____ **(want) to do a concert in another country.**

Well, if it wasn't too far, I 10) _____ (travel) by train. I love trains.

5 Complete the second sentence so that it means the same as the first.

1 We can't go to the concert because we haven't got tickets.
If we _____ _had_ _____ tickets, we could go to the concert.

2 I'd speak to Anna, but she isn't at home.
If Anna _____ at home, I would speak to her.

3 I don't dance when the music isn't very good.
I _____ if the music was better.

4 The theatre is closing because it doesn't make enough money.
If the theatre _____ more money, it wouldn't close.

5 She isn't in the choir because she hasn't got enough time.
If she had more time, she _____ in the choir.

6 We don't practise in this room because it's too small.
If this room was bigger, we _____ in it.

LISTENING

1 🔊 7.1 Listen to the speakers (1–7) and choose the correct answer, A, B or C.

1 What does the boy want to buy?

A   (B)   C

2 What time does the talent show start on TV?

A   B   C

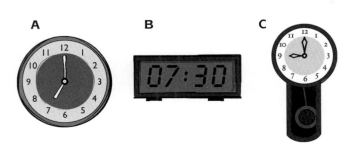

3 Where's Anne's costume?

A  B C

4 What instrument does the girl play now?

A B C

5 What is the boy going to do?

A B C

6 What does the boy want to buy today?

A B C

7 How much does a day ticket for the festival cost?

A B C

£45 £85 £30

GRAMMAR
Subject questions and object questions

1 Read the sentences, then choose the correct words in the questions.

1 Rita Ora wrote that song.
What/Who wrote that song?
2 The ticket fell on the floor.
What/Who fell on the floor?
3 The choir came onto the stage.
What/Who came onto the stage?
4 The costumes were fantastic.
What/Who were fantastic?
5 The exit was difficult to find.
What/Who was difficult to find?
6 The bad weather ruined the festival.
What/Who ruined the festival?

2 Complete the questions with *do, does, did* or –.

1 What _____ *did* _____ you record last month?
2 Who _____ interviewed you for the magazine?
3 What _____ happened at the festival?
4 Who _____ she usually sing with on stage?
5 What _____ they see at the theatre last night?
6 What _____ helps them relax before a concert?
7 What _____ they want to do today?
8 Who _____ plays an instrument?

3 Make questions for these answers.

1 who / teach / you / play the guitar / ?
Q: _____*Who taught you to play the guitar?*_____
A: My dad taught me to play the guitar.

2 what / your friends / think about your music / ?
Q: _____
A: My friends think my music's great.

3 who / write / your songs / ?
Q: _____
A: I write all of them.

4 what / be / the first song / you wrote / ?
Q: _____
A: The first song that I wrote was 'Thunder'.

5 who / you / listen to / when you were at school / ?
Q: _____
A: I listened to Jay'z … all the time.

6 what / you / buy / with the money from your first album / ?
Q: _____
A: I bought a new guitar!

7 what / make / you special / ?
Q: _____
A: My music makes me special. It's different.

SPEAKING SKILLS

1 Put the sentences (a–e) into the correct order (1–4). There is one sentence you do not need.

a It's a nice idea but I'm busy tonight. _____
b Why don't we watch a film at the weekend? _____
c All right then. I love shopping! _____
d What about going shopping on Saturday? _____
e Let's go and see the school play tonight. ___1___

2 Complete the conversation. Use one word in each space.

Max: I think we 1) _*should*_ go to a rock festival this summer.
Emily: I'm not very 2) _____ on rock music.
Max: Then what 3) _____ going to a dance festival?
Emily: I'm 4) _____ I can't because I haven't got enough money.
Max: Well, I think we should do something. 5) _____ don't we organise a beach party?
Emily: That 6) _____ brilliant!

WRITING

1 Match the parts of a review (1–4) with the paragraphs (A–D) to put them in the correct order.

1 Introduction ___C___
2 Positive points _____
3 Negative point _____
4 Conclusion _____

A The costumes in the show are brilliant. They were probably very expensive to make. The best thing is the dancing. Some of the dancers fly across the stage. At the end of the show everybody in the audience was laughing and clapping. It was amazing.

B On the whole, I would recommend this show because it's great fun.

C Last week I went to see the musical 'Wicked' at the Palace Theatre. The audience was full of young and old people and the show lasted for two and a half hours.

D The only bad thing about the show was the heat in the theatre. It was boiling hot.

2 Complete the review with these phrases.

> a fantastic voice   Her songs are fun
> I would recommend   quite expensive
> ~~the new album~~   the price

I've just bought 1) _*the new album*_ by Taylor Swift. It's called 'Red'. I bought it online. My favourite song is called 'Stay, stay, stay'. Taylor Swift has got 2) _____ and she writes lots of her own songs. 3) _____ and I love dancing to her music. The only problem with the album is 4) _____ . I paid £9.59 for it and that's 5) _____ for me. On the whole 6) _____ this album because every track is really good.

3 Put the questions in a review (a–d) into the correct order (1–4).

a What's not so good about it? _____
b What's good about it? _____
c Would you recommend it? _____
d What's the review of? ___1___

4 Write a review of your favourite TV programme. Write about 100–110 words.

08 Going away

READING

1 Read the magazine article. Choose what it is about.

1 a past holiday
2 holidays in general
3 holiday plans

WHAT MAKES YOUR HOLIDAY SPECIAL?
Four readers tell us what they think.

Nathan, 14
❝ Definitely the journey! It's always the most exciting part of the holiday. I love trains and planes but car and bus journeys can be boring if there are traffic jams. ❞

Sophie, 15
❝ I think it's the people that you travel with. Sightseeing and shopping are great fun but I wouldn't like to be on my own in a strange place. ❞

Liam, 16
❝ Going abroad isn't important for me but I like to try something new when I'm on holiday. There are usually lots of activities where I live so I'm happy to be here. ❞

Hannah, 16
❝ I like to have good weather when I'm on holiday. I also love hearing different languages. I often try to learn a few phrases before I go so that I can make friends. ❞

2 Read the article again. Match the names in the article with the online updates (1–4).

💬 View previous comments   Cancel   Share   Post

It's brilliant here. Each day I can choose something different to do. Yesterday I had a climbing lesson. Today, I'm in an arts and crafts class because my legs are hurting after climbing! Tonight some of my new friends are coming to my house. Who needs to go abroad?
    Liam

It was raining when we arrived but this morning it's sunny. The people in the hotel are really friendly and there's a family with a girl who's my age. I said 'hello' to her this morning and she understood me. We're going to the hotel swimming pool later so I hope to see her there.

After a good journey we finally arrived. I'm beginning to make new friends and we've had a fun trip to a castle. I'm glad I'm not on my own because I can't understand the language. Luckily I'm with some great people and we're all getting on really well. This afternoon we're going to buy some souvenirs.

Tonight the train's travelling over the border and we've just stopped to show our passports. It's freezing cold outside but you can see the snow on the mountains. Each day we visit a different town. Then we get back on the train, which is what I like most about this holiday.

Write a comment   Support

VOCABULARY
Travel

1 Choose the correct definition, A or B.

1 destination
   A The place that you come from.
   B The place that you are travelling to.

2 flight
   A A journey by plane.
   B A journey by ferry.

3 border
   A The line that separates two countries.
   B The land next to the sea.

4 motorway
   A A narrow road in the countryside.
   B A wide road for driving fast over long distances.

5 passport
   A A small official book with your photo that you use to travel abroad.
   B A piece of paper that you buy to travel somewhere or to go to an event.

6 sightseeing
   A Visiting famous or interesting places.
   B Buying things, usually in shops.

7 traffic jam
   A A large space where people leave cars.
   B A long line of cars on the road, often moving very slowly.

2 Complete the sentences with travel words. The first letter has been given.

1 She didn't enjoy the f*light* to New York because the plane was hot and noisy.

2 This snow is going to d_____ the bus and we'll arrive late.

3 The j_____ home took eight hours and it was very boring.

4 The planes can't l_____ on this island because there are too many mountains.

5 We're going on a t_____ to Disneyland. I can't wait!

6 Will and his friends are going to t_____ around Europe by train this summer.

3 Choose the correct words.

1 We had a four-hour _delay_/flight before the plane left.

2 The train crosses the abroad/border between Germany and Poland.

3 We heard about the traffic jam/destination on the news so we left early.

4 Jack's gone abroad/sightseeing for the first time. He's never left his country before.

5 The plane can't land/take off until the pilot arrives.

6 Our class is going on a trip/journey to the beach.

4 Match the photos (A–F) with the messages (1–6).

1 Guess who's forgotten their passport? _C_

2 We can't check in until 10 pm #alongwait _____

3 I've been in a traffic jam for three hours ☹ _____

4 The plane's going to take off soon. _____

5 I'm finally leaving the motorway #goinghome _____

6 His plane lands in ten minutes. _____

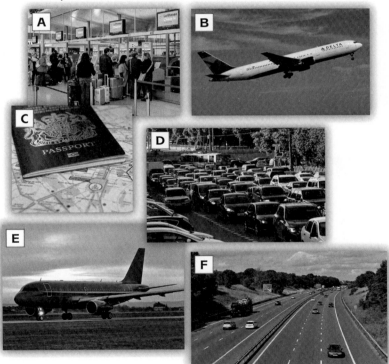

5 Read the sentences. Decide if the underlined word is a noun (n) or a verb (v).

1 I don't think the plane can <u>land</u> in this weather. _v_

2 I was frightened during the <u>take-off</u> because the plane made a loud noise. _____

3 Emily met some friends on the train <u>journey</u>. _____

4 One day I want to <u>travel</u> around the world. _____

5 After a long <u>delay</u> they finally announced our flight. _____

6 Put the letters in the correct order to make travel words. Find the hidden message.

1 n a l d → `l a n d` (4 "land", with box 4 under 'n')

1 n a l d → l a n d (number 4 under third box 'n')

2 e a d y l → □□□□□ (3 under second box)

3 d a b o r a → □□□□□□ (10 and 8 under boxes)

4 n y u r e j o → □□□□□□□ (6 under one box)

5 r o t s a p s p → □□□□□□□□ (12 and 7 under boxes)

6 h i e t n g e s g i s → □□□□□□□□□□□ (11, 1, 9, 5 under boxes)

7 s i t n i t e n a d o → □□□□□□□□□□□ (2 under a box)

Hidden message:
□ □ V □   □   □ □ □ □   □ □ □ □
1 2 3 4   5   6 7 8   9 10 11 12

7 Complete the email with these words.

abroad   flights   journey   motorway
passport   sightseeing   travel   ~~trip~~

mailbox

Today | Mail | Calendar | Contacts

Reply | Reply All | Forward | Delete
From: Daniel   Subject: School trip

Hi Maria
Guess what? I'm going on a school 1) _trip_ to Istanbul. I've already started planning what I need for the long 2) _____ . We're going to 3) _____ by coach because the 4) _____ are very expensive. It's going to take 36 hours! I don't know how much I will see because we'll be on the boring 5) _____ most of the time. I've just found my 6) _____ with a very embarrassing photograph in it. This will be my first holiday 7) _____ because we usually go camping in the mountains near where we live. I can't wait to go 8) _____ and want to visit the Topkapi Palace. I'll send you some photos.
Bye for now
Daniel

8 Choose the best answer, A, B or C.

1 A lot of people are waiting to _____ their bags at the airport.
   A delay   **B** check in   C take off

2 During the two-hour _____ we watched a film.
   A flight   B border   C motorway

3 Oliver heard about the _____ so decided to go by bike.
   A border   B motorway   C traffic jam

4 Today the students are _____ in London, but tomorrow they begin their classes.
   A travelling   B abroad
   C sightseeing

5 Alice enjoyed her holiday in Brazil, but she's very tired after the long _____ home.
   A journey   B trip   C travel

6 I'm always very nervous during the _____ , but when the plane is in the air, I'm fine.
   A delay   B take-off   C check-in

GRAMMAR
Defining relative clauses

1 Put the words in the correct order to make sentences.

1 is / the / that / bag / I / yesterday / bought / This / .
   This is the bag that I bought yesterday.

2 Emma / looking for / flight / a / that / in / stops / is / Paris / .

3 staying / my / with / live / cousins / Canada /who / in /We're / .

4 The / that / very / know / are / students / funny / we / .

5 That's / won / competition / boy / who / the / the / .

6 is / friend / visiting / a / he / who / on / holiday / met / Liam / .

2 Add *who* or *which/that* to complete the sentences where necessary.

1 I've got a new rucksack ___*which*___ is perfect for camping.
2 Anna enjoyed the trip _____ her friends organised for her birthday.
3 There's a boy in my class _____ speaks five languages.
4 The sightseeing trip _____ we booked was brilliant.
5 I live in a town _____ is near the border with Poland.
6 Max can't find the photo _____ he needs for his passport.
7 I get on well with my brothers _____ also love travelling.
8 I know somebody _____ always arrives late.

3 Choose the correct words.

1 Do you remember the girl *who/which* sat next to us on the plane?
2 The city *who/that* I want to visit is Buenos Aires.
3 We're travelling on the train *who/which* goes to Dublin.
4 The people *who/which* work here are very friendly.
5 Where are the tickets *who/which* I gave you this morning?
6 There was a long delay at the airport *who/that* made people angry.

4 Read the sentences. Decide if *who/which/that* refers to the object (O) or the subject (S).

1 We were in a traffic jam *that* lasted five hours. _S_
2 The motorway *which* they used was very busy. _O_
3 That's my neighbour *who* works at the airport. _____
4 I've got a friend *who* has won a holiday in New York. _____
5 What's the name of the website *that* I can use to buy a cheap flight? _____
6 The teachers are planning a trip *which* the students will love. _____
7 The man *who* looked at my passport laughed at the photo. _____
8 The tourists *that* we saw at the check-in were very impatient. _____

5 Complete the blog with *who, which, that* or – . Sometimes more than one answer is possible.

holidayblog.com ⇦ ⇨

💬 View previous comments   Cancel Share Post

Do you want a holiday
1) ___*which/that*___ offers you something different and exciting? You should go on an International Summer Camp! I tried one last year and had a holiday
2) _____ I will never forget. Now I've got friends 3) _____ come from all around the world. Each day you do different activities 4) _____ you choose from an amazing programme. You learn with teachers 5) _____ are experts in their activity. I tried activities 6) _____ were completely new for me, like sky-diving and film-making. At first I was very nervous, but I soon found friends 7) _____ were doing the same activities. The weekends were more relaxing, with sightseeing and shopping trips. One day we met some friends in the town 8) _____ invited us to their party. It was brilliant!

Write a comment   Support

LISTENING

1 🔊 8.1 Listen to the introduction to a radio programme. Choose what the programme is about.

1 summer camp for teens
2 the weather
3 teen travel

2 🔊 8.2 Listen to the rest of the programme. Complete the notes.

Travel company has won a prize for its 1) ___*summer*___
2) _____ .
Name of company: 3) _____ for 4) _____
Type of transport: 5) _____
Maximum number of people on each trip:
6) _____
Accommodation on weekend trips: clean but cheap
7) _____ 8) _____ hotel.
Amount of spending money each student should bring for day trip: 9) £_____
Date of first day trip: 10) _____

GRAMMAR
must, have to

1 Match the sentences (1–6) with the sentences (A–F).

1 You must get a passport. _C_
2 There's a lot of snow on the road. _____
3 We don't have to go sightseeing now. _____
4 They have to go now. _____
5 Jake will be late because of the traffic jam. _____
6 You mustn't leave your bag there. _____

A Somebody might take it.
B We must drive slowly.
C You can't travel abroad without it.
D We have to start without him.
E The train leaves in ten minutes.
F Everything is open tomorrow.

2 Complete the sentences with these verbs.

> didn't have to   ~~don't have to~~   had to
> 'll have to   must   mustn't

1 You _don't have to_ buy the tickets online, but they're cheaper.
2 The train stopped at the border because we _____ show our passports.
3 I _____ see the doctor. I've had a headache for two days.
4 We _____ be late. The bus will leave without us.
5 Alice _____ travel on her own. She met an old friend on the train.
6 The flight leaves tomorrow at 6 a.m. We _____ get up very early.

3 Complete the conversation with the best answer, A, B or C, for each space.

José: Hi Maria, are you ready for your holiday?
Maria: No, not at all. My passport's only just arrived. I 1) _had to_ get a new one because I lost my old one.
José: That's typical of you, Maria. When do you 2) _____ leave?
Maria: We're flying at seven o'clock in the morning so we 3) _____ be at the airport by five o'clock. Dad says we 4) _____ leave the house early in case there's a traffic jam.
José: But you hate getting up early!
Maria: I know. I 5) _____ forget to set my alarm. Anyway, I'm going to pack my bags and then I'm going to bed.
José: That's a pity. I'm just going to Anna's party.
Maria: Anna's party? Hang on, let me think. I 6) _____ pack now.
José: Yes, you do Maria. You can go to the party, but you 7) _____ pack first. I'll come and help. We 8) _____ be there until nine o'clock.
Maria: Brilliant. I hate packing, but I'll do it faster if you help me.

1 A 'll have to
  (B) had to
  C must
2 A have to
  B must
  C will have to
3 A had to
  B don't have to
  C 'll have to
4 A mustn't
  B had to
  C must
5 A don't have to
  B mustn't
  C must
6 A didn't have to
  B don't have to
  C must
7 A had to
  B have to
  C don't have to
8 A mustn't
  B didn't have to
  C don't have to

SPEAKING SKILLS

1 Complete the conversation. Use these sentences.

> Did you have to wait there?
> Oh no, what happened?
> ~~No, you didn't. Was it good?~~
> Really. That's scary.

Liam: Did I tell you about our trip to the Natural History Museum?

Sonia: 1) _No, you didn't. Was it good?_

Liam: It was a disaster. We didn't get there.

Sonia: 2) _____

Liam: Well, we were on the motorway when the driver told us there was a problem with the coach.

Sonia: 3) _____

Liam: Yes, it was. We had to stop at a motorway café and the driver called for another coach.

Sonia: 4) _____

Liam: Yes, we did. The coach took four hours to arrive and in the end we had to come home.

2 Complete the conversation. Use these phrases.

> I lost my friends   It was embarrassing!
> Was it really busy?   How did you find them?
> Who did you go with?   a group of friends
> How did that happen?   ~~We've just been~~

A: 1) _We've just been_ to Aqualandia. It was brilliant.

B: Really? 2) _____

A: I went with 3) _____ from school.

B: 4) _____

A: Yes, it was. Lots of people were there. 5) _____ at one point.

B: You lost your friends? 6) _____

A: Well, I went to buy an ice cream and I forgot where they were sitting.

B: That's awful. 7) _____

A: They saw me and they all started shouting ... very loud. 8) _____

WRITING

1 Complete the holiday blog. Use these phrases.

> a good holiday   ~~something different~~   choose activities
> good ideas for holidays   boat trip   go shopping

> 💬 View previous comments   Cancel   Share   Post
>
> Last year I went on holiday to Venice with my parents and my brother. Each day we did 1) _something different_. My brother wanted to go on a 2) _____, my mum and dad wanted to visit an art gallery and I wanted to 3) _____ for a carnival costume. When you are planning a holiday you have to 4) _____ that everybody likes. Then you all have 5) _____. Have you got any 6) _____? Let me know.

2 Put the sentences in this holiday blog (a–e) into the correct order (1–5).

a In the evenings I go into town with my cousins. ____

b It's busy on the farm in summer and I enjoy helping. ____

c In the summer I always visit my cousins who live on a fruit farm in the country. _1_

d What do you like doing when you're on holiday? I'd love to know. ____

e Sometimes there are street parties with dancing. I love dancing on holiday. ____

3 Read another holiday blog. Put the information (a–e) in the order it appears (1–5).

>
>
> Every summer I go to Mar del Plata with my family. We always go there because my family's got an apartment near the beach. We spend the day swimming and in the evening we usually invite friends to dinner. Everybody has a good time because we've made lots of friends. Do you like making new friends on holiday? Let me know what you think.

a Who is on holiday. ____

b Why they go there. ____

c Why they enjoy it. ____

d Where the holiday is. _1_

e What activities they do. ____

4 Write your own holiday blog. Write about 60 words and ask your reader a question at the end.

Revision Units 7 – 8

VOCABULARY

1 Complete the crossword.

1 R	E	V	I	2 E	W

Across

1 Write a report about a new film, book, etc.

4 Arrange to have or do something at a particular time

6 The way out of a place

7 A group of people who sing together

8 Hit your hands together to show that you enjoyed something

Down

2 Do something that other people like watching or listening to

3 Ask someone questions

5 A group of people who play instruments together

2 Choose the best answer, A, B or C.

1 We tried to _____ a seat for the theatre, but there weren't any left.
  A perform   **B** book   **C** review

2 Emma's rock band is going to _____ an album this summer.
  A entertain   **B** film   **C** record

3 I always sit near the front _____ at the theatre so that I can see everything.
  A stage   **B** row   **C** exit

4 I've got to _____ this book for my English class, but I haven't read it yet.
  A review   **B** perform   **C** interview

5 Jake's left the _____ because he doesn't want to play the violin any more.
  A choir   **B** orchestra   **C** stage

6 This is the same _____ that I wore for the school play last year.
  A stage   **B** audience   **C** costume

3 Complete the sentences with these words.

> check-in   delay   flight   journey
> ~~sightseeing~~   take-off   traffic jam

1 You need at least a week for _sightseeing_ in New York because there are so many interesting places to visit.

2 It was a very boring car _____ so my brother and I started to play silly games.

3 If there's a _____ with our train we'll have time to go to the café for lunch.

4 Nick arrived late at the airport and the _____ desk was closed.

5 We didn't enjoy the _____ because it was a small plane and the seats weren't comfortable.

6 Let's walk home. There's a long _____ in the centre of town and it will be quicker than going by bus.

7 I like the _____ best, especially when the plane climbs above the clouds.

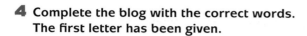

4 Complete the blog with the correct words. The first letter has been given.

View previous comments   Cancel Share Post

Thursday
My new 1) p*assport* finally arrived with its silly photo and now I'm getting ready for my first holiday 2) a_____. I'm going to Carcassonne in the south of France. The town is near the 3) b_____ with Spain so I hope to practise my French and Spanish. We've got a 4) f_____ to Toulouse, but then we have to travel by car to Carcassonne. Mum says it will be a quick 5) j_____ because the 6) m_____ are very good in France. We've got to 7) c_____ _____ for the flight at 3.45 a.m. so I have to start packing now. I can't wait. This time tomorrow I will be 8) s_____ in Carcassonne. There are lots of exciting places to visit, including a very old castle.

Write a comment   Support

GRAMMAR

1 Complete the conversation with the correct form of the verbs in brackets.

Ben: If somebody 1) _bought_ (buy) you a holiday anywhere in the world, where _would you go_ (you / go), Amelia?

Amelia: I'd go to New York. If I 2) _____ (be) there in winter, I _____ (stay) near Central Park.

Ben: Yes, and you could go ice-skating.

Amelia: Exactly! I 3) _____ (not like) it if I _____ (be) on my own.

Ben: If you 4) _____ (can) take a friend, who _____ (it / be)?

Amelia: Phoebe. If she 5) _____ (come) too, we _____ (have) great fun.

Ben: 6) _____ (you / go) shopping if you _____ (be) in New York?

Amelia: Maybe. If we 7) _____ (have) lots of money, we _____ (book) tickets for the theatre every night.

2 Choose the correct words.

1 Who/*What* caused the delay at the airport?
2 Who/What did you interview last night?
3 Who/What found your passport?
4 Who/What was the play about?
5 Who/What did the choir sing?
6 Who/What was at the check-in desk?
7 Who/What bought the tickets?
8 Who/What happened on the motorway?

3 Join the sentences. Use *who*, *that* or *which*. Sometimes more than one answer is possible.

1 I enjoyed the play. We saw it at the theatre.
I enjoyed the play that/which we saw at the theatre.
2 These are the tickets. They cost £20.
3 I've got a friend. She wants to be a pilot.
4 I liked the actor. He was wearing a gold costume.
5 Have you seen the passport? It arrived today.
6 That's the girl. She was ill on the flight.

4 Complete the letter with these verbs.

didn't have to   don't have to   had to   ~~must~~
mustn't   will have to

🌀 **Mill Bank School**

Dear parents and students,
<u>School trip to the Parkland Festival</u>
All students 1) _must_ be at the school at 7.30 a.m. This is important because the coach leaves at 8 o'clock. Last year some students arrived late and 2) _____ travel by train.
Please remember that students 3) _____ eat on the coach. However, the coach will stop on the motorway so that students can have lunch.
The coach will park near the festival site. At the end of the festival, students 4) _____ return to the car park.
Students 5) _____ take bags or coats to the festival. They can leave them on the coach.
Please bring a passport or a student identity card.
Students 6) _____ show them last year, but it's a good idea to take them.
We hope everybody has a great day.
Mr Hiller
Head Teacher

Weird and wonderful world

READING

1 Read the article. Put the paragraphs in the correct order (1–5).

A When I was young I travelled quite a lot with my parents. My dad's a travel writer and we visited lots of different countries. Dad was always working so my mum and I used to go sightseeing. I was mad about photography and started taking photos. One day Dad told me that he wanted to use my photos in his book. Over the next few years I took photos of the Colosseum in Rome, Big Ben in London, the Eiffel tower in Paris and lots more. When my friends saw my photos on the Internet, they said that they were really good. ☐

B Hobbies have improved my life and now I'm doing something that I love. Each weekend, I hang out at the theatre with some great people and we make things. Life's never boring. ☐

C I soon decided that I could do more with the photos. So I began to use them to make models of the buildings I had seen. The first model that I made was of the leaning tower of Pisa. I used anything that I could find at home, put it together with lots of glue and painted it! I always copied the photograph very carefully. Mum said I worked harder on my models than I did on my homework. ☐

D At Hobby News we're always keen to hear about your hobbies and we're often surprised by how creative you are. We've found teens with a passion for collecting anything from old books to key rings. We've also met a talented teen who's mad about cooking and has written his own cookbook. This month we spoke to Dan Hibberd who enjoys taking photos and making models. Dan told us his exciting story. ☐ 1

E Then, one night I went to see a show at the theatre. At the end the theatre manager told the audience that she needed people to help make the furniture and the props for the stage. My dad said it was the perfect job for me, so I offered to help. I help paint the scenes behind the stage and I make the props. The most exciting model I made was of a fountain. At the moment I'm painting a scene at the back of the stage. The theatre is showing the musical 'New York' and I've found some of my photos of the Empire State building and copied them. ☐

2 Read the article and choose the correct answer, A, B, C or D.

1 What's the article about?
   A New and exciting hobbies.
   B Dan's holidays with his parents.
   C Dan's unusual models.
   D How hobbies can change your life.

2 Why did Dan travel a lot when he was young?
   A His dad's job took them to different countries.
   B He wanted to see famous buildings.
   C His mum loved sightseeing.
   D His dad wanted Dan to take photos for him.

3 How did Dan's dad feel about the job in the theatre?
   A He didn't think Dan had the right skills.
   B He thought it was right for Dan.
   C He wanted Dan to do something different.
   D He thought Dan shouldn't get the job.

4 What's Dan's attitude to hobbies?
   A They've made his life better and he enjoys doing them.
   B They've helped him to find an interest in the theatre.
   C They've often stopped him from finding the right job.
   D They've given him the chance to be creative and meet people.

VOCABULARY
Hobbies and interests

1 Match the words (1–7) with the words (a–g) to make hobbies and interests.

1	collecting	a	a musical instrument
2	doing	b	drama
3	keeping	c	fit
4	making	d	gaming
5	making	e	jewellery
6	online	f	key rings
7	practising	g	models

2 Write the names of the hobbies.

1 *cooking*

2 ....

3 ....

4 ....

5 ....

6 ....

3 Choose the correct words.

1 The only problem with my new camera is the *screen/battery*. It doesn't last long.

2 Jack's gone to buy a new *paintbrush/glue*. He's got an art exam tomorrow.

3 I've broken a cup. Perhaps I can repair it with some *glue/pastry*.

4 Amelia went to buy the *ingredients/recipe* for a chocolate cake, but she forgot the flour.

5 I didn't use the *zoom lens/screen* for this photo so you can't really see people's faces.

6 Have you got any *ingredients/scissors*? I want to cut this funny picture out of the magazine.

4 Complete the sentences with these words and phrases.

chill out   ~~keeping fit~~   hang out with
ingredients   join in   taking photos

1 Liam and his brother are into *keeping fit* . They both want to teach sport one day.

2 I didn't feel well on the school trip and couldn't .... the fun.

3 We haven't got the right .... to make a salad. I'll have to go shopping.

4 In the school holidays I usually .... other friends who make models.

5 The girls are mad about .... They never go out without their cameras.

6 You look very tired. You should .... at home before you go to piano practice.

5 Find eight hobby words. Write them under the correct heading.

i	d	n	h	r	p	g	e	e	s	h
n	r	r	s	s	a	t	l	p	s	i
g	n	e	a	i	c	c	t	u	e	c
r	b	c	c	s	s	r	r	p	e	o
e	e	i	h	i	b	b	a	h	i	r
d	s	p	a	s	t	r	y	r	n	o
i	s	e	s	n	s	r	r	e	s	y
e	e	t	i	a	o	t	e	n	o	d
n	b	a	t	t	e	r	y	t	e	p
t	p	i	c	e	c	c	e	c	i	r
s	c	i	s	s	o	r	s	t	r	s

Cooking	Making models	Photography
ingredients		

6 Write the letters in the correct order to make hobby words and complete the sentences.

1 If you have a computer, *online gaming* (elionn mggnia) is brilliant and you can play with all your friends.

2 Have you got anything that I can use to clean the dirty .... (enrsec) on this camera?

3 Nathan enjoys .... (onicokg), but he's really bad at it. That cake was terrible.

4 Max wants to .... (onij ni) the dancing, but he's too embarrassed.

5 The students always enjoy .... (igdno aardm) after school and there are some great actors in the group.

6 I need some strong .... (egul) so that I can repair my skateboard.

7 I can't play an .... (usenrtimnt) but I can sing.

8 Don't use those .... (iossssrc) to cut Lily's hair. Use the sharp ones.

7 Complete the email with these words and phrases.

> are mad about   ~~chill out~~   hang out with
> join in the fun   keeping fit   'm into
> online gaming

Subject: **How was your weekend?**

Hi Kieran

How was your weekend? Did you 1) _chill out_ after your exam on Friday? I went to the beach. Some of my friends 2) _____ taking photos, so we took some cool pictures of the beach in winter. On Saturday it rained all day, but my cousins were here. We all enjoy 3) _____ so we spent a lot of time on the computer. My little sister wanted to 4) _____ , but she was really annoying! I was glad it was sunny yesterday because I 5) _____ skateboarding at the moment and I wanted to go to the new skateboarding park. It's a great place to 6) _____ other skateboarders and I've made lots of friends. 7) _____ is really important and I think skateboarding is a good way to get exercise. Let's go together soon.
Bye for now
Laura

8 Complete the class survey about students' hobbies. Use one or two words in each space.

How do you spend your free time? We've found out some exciting facts about your hobbies and interests. Read the results of our class survey of 15 students.

5 people in the class have never tried 1) _making models_ as a hobby and think that sticking things together with 2) _____ and then painting them can be boring. The rest said they enjoy it and have created robots, aeroplanes and mini animals.

6 people in the class regularly 3) _____ a musical instrument and **3** of them play the electric guitar. The other students in the class would like to buy one, but think they are too expensive.

10 students say that they are 4) _____ taking photos, especially with their mobile phones. Only **4** students prefer to use a real camera. **1** student has just bought a 5) _____ because she enjoys taking close up photos of the fish that she keeps at home.

8 students enjoy 6) _____ unusual things, from old keys to stamps from around the world and even old shoes!

The two most popular hobbies are 7) _____ (if somebody else buys the ingredients!) and 8) _____ , although it's only fun if you've got a good computer and your friends are playing.

The most popular way to spend your free time is with friends. **15** out of **15** students agree that hanging 9) _____ friends after school is the best way to have fun.

GRAMMAR
Reported statements

1 Put the words in the correct order to make sentences.

1 said / Luke / that / the / delicious / cake / was / .
   Luke said that the cake was delicious.

2 would / said / beach / that / They / be / at / they / the / .
   _____

3 bored / girls / they / that / were / The / said / .
   _____

4 We / that / we / make / would / a / said / cake / .
   _____

5 fit / You / me / you / that / told / keeping / loved / .
   _____

6 her / Emma / the / sister / she / couldn't / that / use / camera / told / .
   _____

2 Read the first sentence. Choose the correct words in the reported sentences.

1 'I love making models.'
Nathan _said_/told that he loved making models.

2 'I don't want to do drama.'
Will said that he _didn't want/wanted_ to do drama.

3 'I can't go to your party, Kate.'
I _said/told_ Kate that I couldn't go to her party.

4 'I'll make some jewellery for you.'
Anna told me that she would make some jewellery for _I/me_.

5 'We often take photos of our friends.'
They said that they often took photos of _our/their_ friends.

6 'We'll practise the piano later.'
They said that they _would/wouldn't_ practise the piano later.

7 'Online gaming with friends is fun.'
She _said/told_ me that online gaming with friends was fun.

3 Complete the sentences with the correct form of _say_ or _tell_.

1 We ___told___ him that his model would win the competition.

2 Isaac _____ that he practised the guitar every day.

3 They _____ they would arrive at eight o'clock.

4 Sophie _____ her friends she would be late.

5 I _____ that I didn't want a party.

6 You _____ me you could do it.

4 Complete the blog with these words.

| him | me | played | said | ~~told~~ | wanted | would |

💬 View previous comments   Cancel   Share   Post

Monday
Parents' evening at school! Mum and Dad have just got back. My music teacher 1) ___told___ my dad that I 2) _____ the guitar really well. Dad 3) _____ that he was really surprised because he and Mum can't play any instruments. Then Dad said that he 4) _____ get me a new guitar. Brilliant.

Tuesday
I told 5) _____ that I could help pay for the guitar, but he said that Granddad 6) _____ to pay for it. 'Why?' I asked. Then he told 7) _____ that Granddad learned to play the classical guitar when he was at school. However, when he was young he never had enough money for a good guitar.

Write a comment   Support

5 Complete the conversation with the correct past form of the verb in brackets.

Nia: Hi Dan. Are you coming to drama class tonight?

Dan: No, I can't. I told my brother Tom I 1) ___would___ (will) go swimming with him.

Nia: But, Dan, the drama teacher said we 2) _____ (have to) be at the last class. Don't you remember? She told us that we 3) _____ (need) to practise the songs together.

Dan: I know, but my parents are working. I told them it 4) _____ (be) my last drama class, but they said that they 5) _____ (not want) Tom to be on his own.

Nia: Oh, that's difficult, but I think I can help. My brother said he 6) _____ (want) to watch basketball on TV tonight. Perhaps you could leave Tom at my house?

Dan: That's a great idea. He told me they 7) _____ (like) the same team.

Nia: No problem, Dan. I said that I 8) _____ (can) help!

6 Complete the reported sentences.

> I'll send you the photos.

1 Harry said that he _would send me_ the photos.

> We can leave.

2 Emma told her friends that _____ leave.

> I'm tired.

3 Dan said that _____ tired.

> We don't have the right ingredients.

4 They said that _____ the right ingredients.

> Our models aren't very good.

5 They said that _____ very good.

> I'll call you later.

6 Alice told me that she _____ later.

LISTENING

1 🔊 **9.1 Listen to some students talking about some interesting facts that they know. Choose the correct answer, A, B or C.**

1 What are the six most common letters in English?
(A) RSTLNE   **B** ERSTAN   **C** RSPLNE

2 What was the first animal to go into space?

A   B   C

3 How many stars can the human eye see at night?
A 1 million   **B** 2000–3000   **C** 200–300

4 What is the truth about hot and cold water?

A   B   C

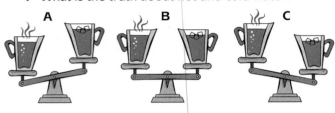

5 How many eyes do bees have?
A 3   **B** 2   **C** 5

6 What should you have if you want to stay awake?

A    B    C

GRAMMAR
used to

1 **Match the sentence beginnings (1–6) with the endings (A–F).**

1 I used to collect stamps, _C_
2 Did you use to do ____
3 Jessica didn't use to like dancing, ____
4 Did they use to watch ____
5 When you were young, did you use to ____
6 Jack didn't use to do sport, ____

A but she loves it now.
B black and white films on TV?
C but I'm interested in other things now.
D but now he plays tennis every day.
E drama after school?
F collect old keys?

2 **Complete the sentences. Use the correct form of *used to* and the verb in brackets.**

1 She _used to enjoy_ (enjoy) keeping fit.
2 Did Max _____ (paint) his models?
3 They _____ (not read) comics.
4 Jessica _____ (write) her own songs.
5 I _____ (not wear) any jewellery.
6 Did they _____ (keep) bees in their garden?

3 Complete the interview. Use the correct form of *used to* and the verb in brackets.

Interviewer: Welcome, Michel. It's great to meet a famous chef. Tell us, 1) *did you use to cook* (you / cook) when you were young?

Michel: Yes, I did. Every summer I 2) _____ (help) my aunt in her hotel. It was only a small hotel, but she 3) _____ (do) all the cooking.

Interviewer: So, did she teach you to cook?

Michel: No, she 4) _____ (not have) much time, but I watched her and that's how I learned.

Interviewer: 5) _____ (you / dream) of becoming a famous chef?

Michel: Not at all! I always wanted to be a famous singer!

Interviewer: A singer?

Michel: Yes, I loved singing in the kitchen of the hotel, but everybody 6) _____ (tell) me to be quiet. I was terrible!

SPEAKING SKILLS

1 Read the sentences (1–6). Choose if they are asking for an opinion (A) or expressing an opinion (E).

1 What do you think about beekeeping? _*A*_
2 I don't agree. _____
3 Yes, I see what you mean but it's weird. _____
4 Why do you think that people collect things? _____
5 I suppose so. _____
6 Do you think it's a good idea? _____

2 Complete the conversations. Use these phrases.

> I don't agree   I see what you mean
> I'm not sure   ~~Why do you think~~
> What do you think about   is a good idea

A: 1) _Why do you think_ that hobbies are important?
B: Because you're never bored when you've got a hobby.
A: Yes, 2) _____ .
A: 3) _____ online gaming?
B: I think it's only fun if you play with friends.
A: 4) _____ . I enjoy it on my own.
A: Do you think doing drama 5) _____ ?
B: 6) _____ . I don't really like it.

WRITING

1 Complete the text. Use these phrases.

> ~~an unusual hobby~~   making models
> it's creative   at primary school
> watches videos   are great

🗨 View previous comments   Cancel   Share   Post

Have you got a friend with 1) _an unusual hobby_ ? My best friend Sam loves 2) _____ of robots. He's made more than two hundred and has always got an idea for a new one.

Sam started making simple models when he was 3) _____ . Then he began to look on the Internet for ideas. He 4) _____ that show you how to make different robots. He loves his hobby because 5) _____ .

Hobbies 6) _____ because they're fun. You can also make lots of friends and share your ideas.

2 Match (1–6) with (a–f) to complete the sentences.

1 Do you know anybody
2 My cousin enjoys
3 He's always made
4 He's good at art and says
5 Cooking is
6 I think hobbies are important

a birthday cakes for the family.
b who likes cooking?
c because they help you relax.
d baking cakes.
e that his cakes are creative.
f a very useful hobby.

3 Complete the notes with these words and phrases.

> because it's fun!   chance to act in plays
> ~~drama~~   drama club   every Friday after school
> gives you confidence

1 The hobby: _____ *drama*
2 Where: _____
3 When: _____
4 What's good about it: _____
5 How it helps you as a person: _____
6 Why you should do it: _____

4 Choose a hobby that interests you but that you don't do. Write about the hobby and say why you would like to do it. Write about 100 words.

READING

1 Read the text quickly and choose the best title, A or B.

A Students find work for a week.

B No jobs for students.

Two years ago, local secondary schools decided to help students gain experience of working life. The schools asked local businesses and companies to take sixteen-year-old students for one week. Students would have the opportunity to find out what skills different jobs need. They could also find out if they were right for a particular job. So how did it go? Did they enjoy the challenge?

Molly

I'm interested in cooking in my free time, so I was really pleased when the school arranged for me to spend a week in a city centre restaurant. I wanted to learn what it was like to work in a busy restaurant. When I arrived on the first day the restaurant was very quiet. First, I had to clean the tables which was quite boring. Then I went into the kitchen and that was completely different. It was very busy because the chef was preparing the menus for lunch and dinner. He explained the different dishes and asked me to check all the ingredients. He told me that in the kitchen it was important to stay calm under pressure. When they started cooking, I began to understand why. People were arriving and they wanted their food – fast. It was hot in the kitchen and the chef was shouting a lot. I did my best to help. At the end of the day I was very tired. Now I'm not sure if I could do that every day.

Jake

I think I'm a creative person but I have no idea what I plan to do in the future. When the school found me a place in a hairdresser's I was quite surprised. However, I enjoy fashion and taking photos so I thought that it was perhaps a good idea. The hairdressers were very friendly and told me about their job. They work long hours but they all said that they enjoyed it. I realised that it's important to be a good team player. So what did I do during the week? I can't cut hair so I had to make coffee for the customers and clean up. I tried to talk to some of the customers but they didn't want to chat because they were reading their magazines. On the last day I learned how to wash hair. Perhaps I'm impatient but I didn't learn much during my week. I don't think it's something that I want to do in the future.

2 Read the text again. Are the sentences (1–10) true (T) or false (F)?

1 Schools wanted students to discover what abilities they needed for a job. _T_

2 The experience didn't teach Jake much. _____

3 Molly enjoys cooking as a hobby. _____

4 Molly enjoyed the first job she did in the restaurant. _____

5 A lot was happening in the kitchen when Molly met the chef. _____

6 Molly didn't know why the chef was shouting. _____

7 Jake's two hobbies are hairdressing and photography. _____

8 The hairdressers all said that they liked their jobs. _____

9 Jake thinks hairdressers should be good at working with others. _____

10 Jake enjoyed chatting to the customers. _____

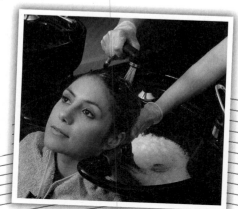

VOCABULARY
Skills for work

1 Match (1–8) with (a–h) to make skills for work phrases.

1	enjoy	**a**	new skills quickly
2	always do	**b**	my/your/his/her/their mind
3	stay	**c**	a challenge
4	make	**d**	my/your/his/her/their best
5	run	**e**	money
6	pick up	**f**	good team player
7	speak	**g**	a business
8	be a	**h**	calm under pressure

2 Put the words in the correct order to make sentences.

1 always / She / challenge / enjoys / a / .
She always enjoys a challenge.

2 important / Making / is / James / money / very / to / .

3 often / They / speak / work / their / at / mind / .

4 good / skills / picking up / at / new / quickly / I'm / .

5 must / your / always / do / best / You / .

6 Dan / run / his / business / sister / a / and / fashion / .

7 you / to / want / be / Do / creative / ?

8 calm / It's / pressure / to / stay / under / difficult / .

3 Choose the correct words.

1 Nathan's doing a course in costume design. He loves being *a good team player/creative*.

2 The course is difficult at the moment, but I *enjoy a challenge/make money* and I'm learning quickly.

3 The hotel is very busy and guests can sometimes be difficult. It's important that you *work on your own/stay calm under pressure*.

4 This summer I'm helping on my uncle's farm. I won't *speak my mind/make money*, but it'll be fun.

5 The problem with Emma is that she always *speaks her mind/does her best*, but sometimes she says too much.

6 In the future I'd like to *work on my own/run a business* with some friends.

4 Complete the advert with the correct words.

CUP CAKE CAFÉ

Cup Cake Café is looking for someone special to join their busy team.

- Are you a good 1) ___team___ player?
- Do you 2) _____ a challenge?
- Can you 3) _____ under pressure?
- Do you always try to 4) _____ your best?
- Would you like to learn how to 5) _____ creative?

If you answered 'yes' to all the above questions, call us now.

Don't worry if you don't have the right experience. Our friendly team will help you to 6) _____ new skills quickly.

5 Complete the words to make eight more negative adjectives.

1	I	P			I		N			
2		N		O	M			T		
3			I		P	S			B	E
4		N		O		R	C			
5	U		S			L				
6	N		X	E		I		E		
7				T			Y			
8	U		F	R		E	D	L		

6 Complete the sentences with the correct adjectives. The prefixes have been given.

1 Your essay is in _complete_ . You've got to finish it before you email it to the teacher.
2 Can you take all your books and bags to your room? This lounge is so un_____ .
3 The hotel manager is angry with Amy because she can be im_____ to guests.
4 I'm trying to phone Dan. I think that the number I've got is in_____ because it won't connect.
5 Hannah designs her own clothes. They're always more un_____ than clothes you buy in the shops.
6 It's im_____ to concentrate in this office because you all talk too much.

7 Complete the sentences with these words and the correct prefix.

> possible   sociable   correct   ~~expensive~~
> friendly   patient   tidy   usual

1 I like going to markets because you can buy _inexpensive_ jewellery and clothes.
2 I'm too _____ to wait for a taxi. It's quicker to walk home.
3 Alice smiled at the customers, but they were _____ and didn't want to talk to her.
4 The receptionist gave me the _____ key for my room and I couldn't open the door.
5 The shop is _____ because the customers look at things and then put them back in the wrong place.
6 It was _____ that Paul arrived late for work. He's often the first person there.
7 It's _____ to keep up with all of the homework this term. Our teacher gives us too much.
8 Being a musician is a fun job, but the hours are very _____ . I'm always working in the evenings.

8 Complete the text with the best answer, A, B, C or D, for each space.

Dream job

I've always wanted to be a vet. I love animals and I don't mind working 1) __on__ my own. Vets work long hours and often have to 2) _____ calm under pressure. Some big animals can be very difficult to work with and others are just 3) _____ and don't like people. I would always 4) _____ my best to help an animal that was sick. A vet's job is quite 5) _____ because they often have to work during the night and sleep during the day, but that isn't a problem for me. I don't want to 6) _____ a business as a vet. I'm not interested in 7) _____ money. I just want to help animals and offer 8) _____ treatment for sick animals.

1	**A** in	**B** on
	C for	**D** at
2	**A** spend	**B** be
	C stay	**D** stop
3	**A** unfriendly	**B** impolite
	C untidy	**D** unusual
4	**A** make	**B** have
	C show	**D** do
5	**A** incomplete	**B** impossible
	C incorrect	**D** unusual
6	**A** run	**B** make
	C work	**D** do
7	**A** enjoying	**B** making
	C doing	**D** working
8	**A** unusual	**B** expensive
	C inexpensive	**D** unfriendly

GRAMMAR
to + infinitive/-ing form

1 Complete the sentences with the full infinitive of these verbs.

> apply   ~~come~~   design   run
> speak   teach

1 Kate's promised ___to come___ to the office this afternoon.
2 I've started _____ my own clothes.
3 It isn't easy _____ your own business at the moment.
4 Charlie and Hanna are learning _____ Russian.
5 Have you decided _____ for the job?
6 One day I want _____ in a primary school.

2 Complete the email. Use the *-ing* form of the verbs in brackets.

> **mailbox**
> ⠀⠀⠀⠀⠀⠀⠀⠀⠀⠀Today Mail Calendar Contacts
>
> Reply | Reply All | Forward | Delete
> From: **Naomi**⠀⠀⠀⠀⠀Subject: **Hi!**
>
> Hi Dan
> Have you finished 1) ___revising___ (revise) for your last two exams? I can't imagine
> 2) _____ (have) two in one day! When you finish you can enjoy 3) _____ (do) nothing for a while.
> Here's a photo of me with my young cousin, Luke. He's doing a summer camp and I'm helping. I'm interested in 4) _____ (work) with children one day so it's good experience.
> Mum says I'm good at 5) _____ (entertain) them because I make them laugh.
> I'm looking forward to 6) _____ (see) you in July. What date are you coming?
> Write soon
> Naomi

3 Choose the correct words.

1 I can't stand *working/to work* on my own. It's boring.
2 Will isn't interested in *making/to make* money.
3 Phoebe wants *selling/to sell* her own clothes.
4 What do you hope *doing/to do* in the future?
5 Harry doesn't mind *staying/to stay* late.
6 It isn't possible *finishing/to finish* this today.
7 Are you looking forward to *travel/travelling* around Europe?
8 I don't enjoy *working/to work* under pressure.

4 Complete the sentences. Use the correct form of the verbs in brackets. Sometimes more than one answer is possible.

1 It's important ___to be___ (be) happy in your job.
2 Alice is good at _____ (bake). She should have a café.
3 They prefer _____ (work) for their dad.
4 Oliver has asked _____ (leave) early.
5 I love _____ (help) on my grandparents' farm.
6 They've arranged _____ (stay) for the summer.
7 We don't mind _____ (be) on our own.
8 The students start _____ (pick up) new skills quickly.

5 Complete the article with these verbs.

> making   meeting   selling   to get
> to help   to run   to speak   ~~working~~

How do you spend your summer? We're interested in hearing your stories. This week *Nick* tells us how he made the most of his holiday.

My parents have a small ice cream shop and last summer I started 1) ___working___ in it. I really enjoyed 2) _____ customers and I was good at 3) _____ things to them. I also learned 4) _____ English well because a lot of the customers were American tourists. I think it's important 5) _____ some work experience before you leave school. One day I hope 6) _____ my own business and Dad's agreed 7) _____ me. I'm really interested in 8) _____ models of boats and I think I could sell them. I am finding out about how to start an online business.

LISTENING

1 🔊 **10.1 Listen to the first part of a radio programme. Choose what the programme is about.**

1 What to do in the summer.
2 How to find a job after school.

2 🔊 **10.2 Listen to the rest of the programme. Choose the correct answer, A, B or C.**

1 What does Rory do at the hotel?
   A He sells gifts.
   (B) He performs for the guests.
   C He sings in the kitchen.

2 What entertainment do the hotel guests like most?
   A Irish music
   B Traditional dancer
   C Disney films

3 Why does Rory have singing lessons?
   A He wants to perform well in the hotel.
   B He knows he has to get better.
   C He hopes to sing on TV one day.

4 What does Rory find interesting about his job?
   A He likes to watch the people in the audience.
   B He often meets famous people.
   C He can learn about different countries.

5 Why does Rory want to find another job?
   A There's no work in the hotel in winter.
   B The hotel doesn't pay enough money.
   C He needs more experience.

GRAMMAR
Indirect questions

1 Put the words in the correct order to make questions.

1 Can I ask you why / job / the / you /enjoy / ?
   Can I ask you why _____ *you enjoy the job?*
2 Do you know when / the / starts / job / ?
   Do you know when _____
3 Do you know if / will / team / be / in / you / a / ?
   Do you know if _____
4 Can you tell us where / you / work / will / ?
   Can you tell us where _____
5 Can I ask how long / here / you / worked / have / ?
   Can I ask how long _____
6 Could you tell us why / do / you / to / wanted / it / ?
   Could you tell us why _____

2 Put the words in brackets in the correct place in the questions.

1 Do you know the job is difficult? (if)
   Do you know if the job is difficult?
2 Can I ask you became a doctor? (why)
   _____
3 Can you tell us you trained? (where)
   _____
4 Can you tell us you stayed? (how long)
   _____
5 Could you tell me you got the job? (how)
   _____
6 Can you tell me I have to do today? (what)
   _____

3 Complete the interview with Sophie, a teenage dress designer. Use the questions in brackets to make indirect questions.

Fashion World

FW: Hi Sophie. I love your dress. Can I ask you 1) _____ *if you made it?* (Did you make it?).

Sophie: Yes, I made it for a friend's party.

FW: Can you tell us 2) _____ (How long does it take to design a dress?)

Sophie: It depends. Sometimes I can design a dress in a day, but sometimes it takes weeks.

FW: Could I ask you 3) _____ (When did you start designing?)

Sophie: When I left school, I did a course in clothes design.

FW: I see, and do you know 4) _____ (Are there many professional teenage designers?)

Sophie: Yes, there are. Some of them are very good.

FW: Do you know 5) _____ (What do you want to do in the future?)

Sophie: Yes, I'd love to run my own business.

FW: That's a great idea. Can I ask you 6) _____ (Have you made a dress for a famous person?)

Sophie: No, I haven't, but I'd like to one day.

FW: Well, good luck, Sophie.

SPEAKING SKILLS

WRITING

1 Put the words in the correct order.

1 looks / a / like / big / It / balloon / .
It looks like a big balloon.

2 round, / that / thing / metal / What's / ?

3 big / looks / It / like / hat / a / .

4 thing / that / his / on / What's / coat / ?

5 thing / the / What's / white / big, / ?

6 like / suitcase / looks / a / It / .

2 Complete the description of a photo. Use the words below.

> like   long   looks   ~~sitting~~
> taking   thing

" They're 1) _sitting_ on a beach. It 2) _____ cold because the boy's wearing a 3) _____ , black scarf. She's got something on her head. It looks 4) _____ a hat from Peru. I think he's 5) _____ a photo with his mobile phone. I'm not sure what they're sitting on. It's a 6) _____ that you often have on the sofa at home. "

1 Complete the formal letter with these phrases. There are two phrases you do not need.

> Bye for now   ~~Dear Sir/Madam,~~   I'm writing to apply
> Hello   I have some experience   I'm a good team player
> I look forward to hearing   Yours faithfully,

1) _Dear Sir/Madam_ ,

2) _____ for the job of volunteer at the High5 Music Festival this summer. I study music at school and would enjoy helping musicians and performers.

   3) _____ but I can also work well on my own. I can stay calm under pressure.

   4) _____ because I helped at our school festival last year. I collected the tickets and served food and drinks in the busy café.

5) _____ from you soon.

6) _____

Sam Johnson

2 Choose the five pieces of information in (1–7) that you should give in an application letter.

① The name of the job you want to apply for.

2 A list of your hobbies.

3 The reason you want the job.

4 A list of things you don't do well.

5 A list of your skills.

6 Details of experience that would be useful.

7 The date when you are free to start work.

3 Put the parts of a letter (A–F) in the correct order (1–6).

A I'm writing to apply for the job of dog walker. I've always loved animals and keeping fit. I would enjoy walking your dogs every day. _____

B Dear Sir/Madam _1_

C I enjoy a challenge. I'm also happy to work on my own and am very patient with animals. I think that these two skills would be very useful. _____

D Yours faithfully, _____

E I look forward to hearing from you soon. _____

F I also have some experience because I walked my friend's dog when she was on holiday and took the dog to the park when she was in hospital. _____

4 Your tennis club needs a volunteer to help in the café during the summer. Write an application letter for the job. Write about 90–100 words.

Revision Units 9 – 10

VOCABULARY

1 Write the letters in the correct order to make hobby words. Complete the mystery sentence.

1 L E U G | G | L | U | E |
               9   2

2 T A P S Y R | | | | | |
                       6

3 N E R C E S | | | | | |
                   16   4   8

4 T A E R Y T B | | | | | | |
                         14   11

5 M O Z O   S E L N | | | | | | | | |
                         3 10 5   12 15 13

6 C E R P I E | | | | | |
                   1

7 S S R O C S S I | | | | | | | |
                       7   17

| | | V | | | | | K | | |
1   2   3   4   5   6   7 8 9

| | D | | | | | | D | |
5 10   11 12 13   14 15

| | K | | | |
16 17 3   1 8 9

2 Choose the correct words.

1 Jack and Dan don't like *keeping fit/<u>online gaming</u>* because they prefer doing sport outside.
2 We haven't got any homework tonight! Let's *chill out/ join in* at the beach.
3 That's a really nice necklace. I didn't know that you liked making *models/jewellery*.
4 There's a festival in the park. Why don't you go and *join in/hang out with* the fun?
5 *Cooking/Doing drama* is great, especially when you can eat the results.
6 Grace is saving for a new camera. She's *mad about/ hanging out with* taking photos.

3 Complete the phrases. There are two words you do not need.

> business ~~challenge~~ creative do
> money on skills speak stay team

1 enjoy a ___challenge___
2 pick up new _____ quickly
3 _____ calm under pressure
4 _____ my mind
5 always _____ your best
6 work _____ their own
7 run a _____
8 make _____

4 Complete the text with the best answer, A, B or C, for each space.

My dad 1) __runs__ a sailing business and in the summer I enjoy helping him. I try to 2) _____ my best, but sometimes I don't know what I'm doing. He's great because he's never 3) _____ with me. He explains things slowly and always encourages me. He says I 4) _____ up new skills quickly. We have lots of customers in the summer, but Dad always stays 5) _____ under pressure. The only problem is the office. It's so 6) _____ because there are papers and books all over the floor. I try to organise it for him and keep it clean, but it's 7) _____ !

1 A makes   **B** runs   C does
2 A do   B work   C speak
3 A unfriendly B incorrect   C impatient
4 A put   B pull   C pick
5 A calm   B quiet   C silent
6 A incomplete B untidy   C unusual
7 A impossible B unfriendly C inexpensive

GRAMMAR

1 Complete the reported sentences.

1 'I'll make a cake,' he said.
   He said that *he would make a cake* .
2 'We can't find any batteries,' they said.
   They said that _____ .
3 'The work in the hotel is interesting,' she said.
   She said that _____ .
4 'I'm mad about taking photos,' Nick said.
   Nick said that he _____ .
5 'My camera isn't working,' Lucy told me.
   Lucy told me that _____ .
6 'Your dinner is ready,' their dad said.
   Their dad told them _____ .
7 'We enjoy doing drama after school,' the girls said.
   The girls said that _____ .
8 'I don't like difficult recipes,' Max said.
   Max said that _____ .

2 Complete the blog with the correct form of *used to* and the verbs in brackets.

💬 View previous comments   Cancel   Share   Post

When you were young 1) *did you use to have*
(you / have) a favourite hobby? I was mad about
collecting things. I 2) _____ (love)
big, old keys and every time I found one I
3) _____ (put) it in a very old box
which I locked with a special key.
I 4) _____ (not do) anything with the
keys. I just 5) _____ (like) looking at
them. I tried to imagine who the key belonged to.
6) _____ (they / live) in a huge house
with a big door? What happened to them?
I 7) _____ (believe) that every key
had its own story.
What about you? Do you have an unusual hobby?
I'd love to hear about it.

Write a comment   Support

---

3 Complete the sentences with the infinitive or the *-ing* form of these verbs.

---

be   help   make   run   speak   stay
take   ~~work~~

---

1 Do you enjoy ___*working*___ on your own?
2 She's good at _____ her own clothes.
3 They hope _____ a computer business one day.
4 Are you interested in _____ photos of animals?
5 Olivia has agreed _____ us in the café this afternoon.
6 I think it's important _____ a good team player.
7 It isn't easy for James _____ his mind.
8 Dan doesn't mind _____ late because he loves his job.

4 Complete the indirect questions.

1 When did you start making websites?
   Can you tell us when ___*you started*___ making websites?
2 Where did you study website design?
   Can I ask you _____ website design?
3 Is it easy to find work?
   Do you know if _____ to find work?
4 What sort of computer have you got?
   Could you tell me what sort of computer _____ ?
5 How long does it take to make a website?
   Can I ask _____ to make a website?
6 Are there many teenage web designers?
   Do you know if _____ many teenage web designers?

Our planet

READING

1 Read the first paragraph of a review. Choose what the review is about.

1 A new film **2** A DVD game **3** A geography book

2 Now read the complete review. Choose the correct answer.

Are you tired of learning geography from books? Then you should try Extreme World. It's a great way to find out about the natural world. You watch a DVD and play a game at the same time. During the game the DVD 1) *answers / replies / asks / demands* you questions about the natural world. You work in teams and 2) *discuss / argue / explain / describe* the options. It's fun because you see videos of places around the world and you learn lots of new things.

The first part of the game is about water. Do you know 3) *who / what / where / why* you can find the highest waterfall in the world? I had no idea but one of my friends has a granddad in Venezuela who has taken him to the Angel Waterfalls in Venezuela. The cliffs are 979 metres high and water drops over them into the Gauja river. He 4) *talked / said / tell / told* us that the waterfall was named after a man called Jimmie Angel. He was the first person who flew over it.

The second part of the game is about weather. In our game my team was asked where the coldest place the world is. We all decided that it was Russia but we didn't know where exactly so we didn't 5) *gain / lose / earn / win* the point. The correct answer is Oymyakon. Sometimes the temperature is as low as -50C. Luckily they do get some sunshine in summer 6) *because / although / as / and / since* the ground is always frozen. Imagine that!

The third part of the game is about mountains. I wanted a question about the highest mountain in the world because I know that it's Everest. 7) *However / So / Also / Still* we were asked about the longest mountain path in the world. We all thought it was in Europe or South America but we were wrong.

It's the Appalachian path in the United States. It's about 3,500 km long and it's famous 8) *for / about / of / with* its big, black bears and poisonous snakes. Scary!

The final part of the game was my favourite. The questions were about the sky and the stars. In fact we were asked how long it takes for the moon to travel 9) *over / around / about / into* the Earth. The rest of my team thought it was 28 days but I knew the answer was 27.3 because I learned it at school. I chose the answer and we won a point.

We played Extreme World for hours. We only got a few questions right in the end, but that was fine. We all 10) *advised / argued / agreed / arranged* the game was fun and we can't wait to play it again. I recommend that you try it too!

VOCABULARY
Natural world

1 Match two squares to make a word. Find nine natural world words and write them under the correct heading.

pa	so	sa
nd	st	cl
mi	cl	mo
th	il	oud
iff	st	ck
ar	on	ro

Sky/weather	Ground
	path

2 Complete the words with *a, e, i, o* or *u*.

1 cl _o_ _u_ d
2 s___nsh___n___
3 w___v___s
4 w___t___rf___ll
5 s___ ___l
6 m___ ___n
7 ___v___l___nch
8 p___th
9 pl___n___t
10 t___mp___r___t___r___
11 ___c___ ___n
12 f___r___st

3 Write the letters in the correct order to make natural world words and complete the sentences.

1 We couldn't see where we were going because the _____mist_____ (stmi) was bad.

2 The ski instructor told them to go home because there was danger of an _____ (vnehalaca).

3 When we saw the high _____ (vsawe) we decided to go surfing.

4 Max was worried when he saw his friends walking along the top of the _____ (fcfil).

5 Grace and her friend were relaxing in the sun when they saw a black _____ (dcolu) in the distance.

6 It's so hot at the beach today that it's impossible to walk on the _____ (ndas).

4 Complete the email with the correct word. The first letter has been given.

Subject: **Camping** ⇦ ⇨ ⌂

Hi Ben
This mountain campsite is fantastic. We arrived late last night, but it was still light because there was a full 1) m_oon_____. You could see hundreds of 2) s_____. It was so cool. This morning there isn't a 3) c_____ in the sky and it's very warm. I hope this 4) s_____ lasts, but I don't think it will. The owner of the campsite says it will be windy tomorrow and there could be a 5) s_____ because they get a lot at the end of the summer. This morning we're going for a walk. There's a 6) p_____ that goes up to a 7) w_____ where we hope to swim. The water will be freezing!
See you soon.
Anna

5 Complete the information in the holiday brochure with these words. There are two words you do not need.

cliff   mist   paths   sand   soil   stars   ~~sunshine~~   waterfall   waves

Island Adventure Centre

Come on your own or come with friends. With around 325 days of 1) _____sunshine_____ every year you won't be bored at Island Adventure Centre! You can surf the 2) _____, play beach volleyball on the soft white 3) _____ or join us on an exciting midnight walk along one of the beautiful mountain 4) _____ that lead to the highest 5) _____ in Turkey. Our adventure centre is located on the top of a 6) _____ with amazing views of the mountains behind and the sea in front. In the evenings we also offer boat trips with music so you can dance all night and watch the 7) _____ in the sky at the same time.

6 Write these adjectives under the correct heading.

~~beautiful~~   blue   dangerous   deep   high
horrible   interesting   new   old   scary

Opinion	Fact
beautiful	

7 Match the sentence beginnings (1–7) with the endings (A–G).

1 They live in a big, _C_
2 Marie's making a wonderful, ...
3 She's wearing a strange, ...
4 They're swimming in a dangerous, ...
5 We're looking at the small, ...
6 I couldn't walk on the hot, ...
7 Harry followed the scary, ...

A blue coat.   E deep lake.
B white stars.   F long path.
C old house.   G chocolate cake.
D black sand.

8 Complete the blog with the best answer, A, B or C, for each space.

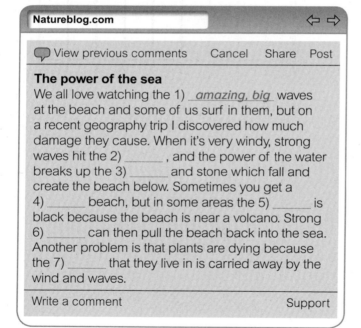

Natureblog.com   ⇦ ⇨

💬 View previous comments   Cancel   Share   Post

The power of the sea
We all love watching the 1) _amazing, big_ waves at the beach and some of us surf in them, but on a recent geography trip I discovered how much damage they cause. When it's very windy, strong waves hit the 2) .... , and the power of the water breaks up the 3) .... and stone which fall and create the beach below. Sometimes you get a 4) .... beach, but in some areas the 5) .... is black because the beach is near a volcano. Strong 6) .... can then pull the beach back into the sea. Another problem is that plants are dying because the 7) .... that they live in is carried away by the wind and waves.

Write a comment   Support

1 A big, amazing   B amazing and big
  C amazing, big
2 A paths   B cliffs   C clouds
3 A rock   B soil   C sand
4 A beautiful, white   B beautiful and white
  C white, beautiful
5 A soil   B sand   C cliff
6 A rocks   B waves   C sunshine
7 A mist   B soil   C rock

GRAMMAR
Present simple passive and past simple passive

1 Choose the correct words.

1 The sand on the beach *is/are* cleaned every morning.
2 This fruit *isn't/aren't* used for cooking because it tastes disgusting.
3 The waterfall *is/are* often photographed at night.
4 The tickets for the trip *isn't/aren't* included in the price of the holiday.
5 Your help *isn't/aren't* needed at the moment.
6 The forest plants *is/are* used to make medicine.

2 Complete the sentence with *was, were, wasn't* or *weren't*.

1 They believe that the avalanche ___was___ caused by the change in temperature.
2 The mystery rock .... discovered until ten years ago.
3 All the sandwiches .... eaten on the long walk in the mountains.
4 Ben and Hannah .... warned about the river, but still went swimming.
5 The moon .... covered by the clouds so we couldn't see it.
6 The animals .... given enough food and they were still hungry.

3 Find nine past participles.

c	e	t	f	o	u	n	d
c	r	e	a	t	e	d	t
b	b	d	l	t	e	t	a
u	o	i	a	k	n	m	e
e	u	e	c	e	t	a	e
b	g	e	k	p	e	d	a
c	h	a	e	t	n	e	e
c	t	k	t	a	e	c	k

4 Complete the sentences. Use the verbs in brackets and the passive form of the tenses given.

1 The tourists ___*are warned*___ (warn) to leave the beach when there's a red flag. (present simple)
2 The children _____ (not teach) in the villages where they live. (present simple)
3 This photo _____ (take) when we were in India. (past simple)
4 More help _____ (need) if we are going to change this situation. (present simple)
5 The rubbish bags _____ (collect) early each morning. (present simple)
6 Dangerous animals _____ (not use) in the documentary. (past simple)
7 The river _____ (clean) by volunteers every year. (present simple)
8 The small houses _____ (build) by their grandparents many years ago. (past simple)

5 Complete the newspaper report with these passive verbs.

> are covered   're told   's believed
> was heard   were given   were told
> ~~were warned~~

Last week tourists in the ski centre of Gretz 1) ___*were warned*___ about the possibility of an avalanche. Guests at the Mountain View Hotel 2) _____ to stay in their rooms. For two days nothing happened. One guest, Mr Hewlett, told us that his kids 3) _____ games and DVDs by the hotel, but they were still fed up. 'Imagine it', he said. 'We're in this beautiful place, the mountains 4) _____ in snow and we can't go out.' Then, on Friday morning, a sound 5) _____ high in the mountains. It was the avalanche. 'It was very scary', said Mr Hewlett. 'Now I know. If you 6) _____ to stay inside, you should stay inside.' It 7) _____ that ten people are still missing.

6 Read the email and complete the sentences. Use the correct form of the passive.

mailbox — Today | Mail | Calendar | Contacts
Reply | Reply All | Forward | Delete
From: **Aiden**   Subject: **Masca**

Dear Charlotte
I'm staying in an amazing village in Tenerife. They call it 'Masca' which means 'hidden'. Local people say that the village was a secret for many years. They didn't discover it until the 1960s. The people in the village built new houses and cafés. Now tourists visit it every day. Unfortunately young people don't need the new houses because they are leaving the village to work in the city. ☹☹
See you soon
Aiden

1 The village ___*is called*___ Masca.
2 It _____ that the village was a secret for many years.
3 The village _____ until the 1960s.
4 A few years ago new houses and cafés _____ .
5 Now, it _____ by tourists every day.
6 The new houses _____ by young people because they're leaving the village.

LISTENING

1 🔊 **11.1 Listen to the conversation. Choose what the people are talking about.**

    1 A camping weekend.
    2 A geography trip.
    3 A summer camp.

2 🔊 **11.2 Listen again. Are the sentences (1–6) true (T) or false (F)?**

    1 At first Max doesn't know if he likes the idea of the Green Camp. *T*
    2 Anna slept well when she was in the mountains. ......
    3 Max and Anna agree that they aren't interested in cooking. ......
    4 Anna isn't keen on the idea of studying the water. ......
    5 Anna and Max like the same things at school. ......
    6 Anna advises Max to do the Green Camp. ......

GRAMMAR
could, should

1 **Are the sentences suggestions (S), advice (A) or strong advice (SA)?**

    1 You should use sun cream when it's sunny.   *A*
    2 We could visit the waterfall today. ......
    3 You could try surfing as the waves are good. ......
    4 You shouldn't wear those shoes on this dangerous path. ......
    5 We could wait for better waves before we go surfing. ......
    6 You should never go walking in the mountains if there's a storm. ......

2 **Choose the correct words.**

Anna: Hi, Mark. It's a lovely day. I think we 1) *should/shouldn't* go swimming in the lake this afternoon.

Mark: No, I don't want to. My dad says you 2) *couldn't/shouldn't* swim there because it isn't clean.

Anna: Oh, that's horrible. Well, we 3) *could/should* go for a walk and enjoy the sunshine.

Mark: OK, but it's very hot. If we go, 4) we *should/could* take lots of water.

Anna: Well, you 5) *could/should* bring the water and I'll get some food.

Mark: All right. Do you think I 6) *should/could* change?

Anna: Mark, of course you 7) *should/could*. You're in your hot school uniform!

SPEAKING SKILLS

1 Complete the conversation. Use these phrases.

> carry on   ~~Shall I go first~~   So, do we agree
> We definitely want to make the most of the day
> What do you think   Yes, we agree   So do I

Anna: OK. 1) _Shall I go first_ ? Well, I think we should leave very early for our trip to the mountains.

James: 2) _____ . I've already found out the times of the trains. There's one at 6.30 that stops near the path that takes us to the waterfall. Am I going too fast?

Charlie: No, 3) _____ .

James: OK. We should all wear boots and take maps, hats, sunglasses and lots of water. It can be cloudy in the mountains but it will still be hot. 4) _____ , Anna?

Anna: I think you're right.

James: 5) _____ that we take the early train?

Anna and Charlie: 6) _____ .

Anna: 7) _____ .

2 Complete the short conversations. Use one word in each space.

1 **A:** Shall I _____go_____ first?
  B: Yes, you begin.

2 **A:** _____ do you think?
  B: I think it sounds great.

3 **A:** So, _____ you agree?
  B: Yes, I do.

4 **A:** Please _____ on.
  B: Thanks. Well, I think we should make posters.

5 **A:** Did you want to say something, Mark?
  B: No, after _____ .

WRITING

1 Read the description. Underline the eight adjectives.

> **If you love the countryside and the beach you should visit the west coast of Ireland.**
> There are <u>beautiful</u> beaches where you can watch dolphins and wonderful paths that take you across the cliffs of Moher.
>   One of the best ways to spend the day is on a boat trip to the stunning Aran Islands. You can't drive a car but there are lots of bikes so that you can cycle around the island. The countryside is fantastic. The local people are very friendly and they speak the Irish language or Gaelic. There are lots of small cafés where local bread and cakes are made. You have to try them. They're delicious!

2 Put the words in the correct order to make sentences.

1 visit / peaceful / You / mountain / the / villages. / should
  You should visit the peaceful mountain villages.

2 horses / on / hills. / are / often / the / Wild / seen /
  _____

3 waterfall. / There's / stunning / a
  _____

4 every / town / visited / by / year. / This / three / tourists / is / million
  _____

5 the / place / perfect / It's / a / holiday. / for
  _____

3 Complete the notes. Use these words and phrases.

> go rock-climbing   in the mountains
> it's fascinating   it's peaceful   listen to local music
> ~~next to a waterfall~~   old castles   wild animals

1 Where is it?
  next to a waterfall , _____

2 What can you see there?
  _____ , _____

3 What can you do there?
  _____ , _____

4 Why should people go there?
  _____ , _____

4 Write a description for a friend of a place that you like. Describe what you can see and do there, and include a variety of adjectives. Write about 100–110 words.

12 Something new!

READING

1 Read the article quickly. Match the people with the photographs (A–C).

Summer Challenge

Are you looking for something that's fun and different? Then why not join us for a three-day super Summer Challenge. Day one offers the creative challenge. Perhaps you like cooking, writing stories or making models? On day two there's a sporting challenge. Don't worry if you're not into sport. This is about taking part and trying something new. Finally, day three is the popular music challenge. Do you want to sing in a choir or play a musical instrument? We want to help you find your hidden talent. Summer Challenge is for teens aged 13–18 and our prices are very reasonable. You'll make lots of new friends but you'll also go home with new skills and a new confidence. Here's what some of last year's participants said:

Laura
I heard about Summer Challenge from a friend who had done it the year before. I've always done a lot of sport but wanted to try something else this summer. The music challenge was amazing. We started the day with some basic voice exercises. I thought they would be boring but the teacher was good and made them fun. At the beginning we were terrible but we laughed a lot and soon we got better. We were put into three groups and each group sang a different part of a song. At the end of the day we performed a short concert. The challenge was life-changing for me. I'd never sung before but now I'm in the school choir and I've got a new group of friends.

Daniel
Writing stories is my hobby so I thought the creative challenge was a great idea. I was in a group with four others and we chose to make a short film. We had to discuss our ideas before we could sort out how to make the film. I'd already written a story at school about bullying. We agreed that we would save time if we used my idea. First we wrote a short play from the story. One of the boys in the group was keen on photography so he filmed it. I directed it and the others were the actors. Although I'm pleased that we used my idea for the film, the most important thing was that we worked as a team. I think that's why we won the prize.

Olivia
I live in very small village where there isn't much to do during summer so I was excited about the Summer Challenge. The best day for me was the sporting challenge. I'm not very keen on team sports like football or volleyball but I like keeping fit. We were offered different activities including climbing, trampolining and free-running! I'd always wanted to try climbing. We worked in teams and encouraged each other from the beginning. It was a really positive experience and I found out I'm really good at it. I'm going to get some climbing equipment and join a club when I go home.

2 Read the text again and choose the correct answer, A, B, C or D.

1 What's the writer doing in the text?
- **A** Complaining about last year's students.
- **B** Explaining why Summer Challenge is cheap.
- **C** Encouraging teens to do the Summer Challenge.
- **D** Advising teens make new friends during the summer.

2 What's the aim of the music challenge?
- **A** To learn to sing well.
- **B** To learn about different musical instruments.
- **C** To perform in a choir for the first time.
- **D** To discover a skill you didn't know you had.

3 Why does Daniel think his group's film won the prize?
- **A** The group made the best film in the time they had.
- **B** The people in the group worked well with each other.
- **C** The group had come up with the best idea for a film.
- **D** The people in the group all had different skills.

4 What did Olivia discover during her challenge?
- **A** She enjoys working in a team.
- **B** She needs to buy some climbing equipment.
- **C** She can climb really well.
- **D** She likes encouraging others.

VOCABULARY
Describing experiences

1 Complete the crossword with adjectives that describe experiences.

(crossword grid with letters: L, I across top row 1; H; T; O across row 6; V; A; and bottom row 7 with T, T, N)

Across
1 difficult but interesting
3 enjoyable
6 good or useful
7 makes you want to do something

Down
2 very tiring
4 difficult and can cause problems
5 makes you feel calm and comfortable

2 Complete the words in the sentences with *a, e, i, o* or *u*.

1 It was a t _o_ _u_ gh competition so James was surprised when he won.
2 Learning to cook was l___f___-ch___ng___ng for me.
3 Amelia said it was ___mb___rr___ss___ng when she dropped her lunch on the floor.
4 After the exams we need a r___l___x___ng day at the beach.
5 The science trip was a p___s___t___v___ experience for the students.
6 Climbing the mountain in the rain was ___xh_____st_____ng.
7 The drama students found the actor's visit to the school very m___t___v___t___ng.
8 The sign language course is ch___ll___ng___ng at first, but most students enjoy it.

3 Match the questions (1–7) with the answers (A–G).

1 Was your party fun, Liam? _D_
2 It's very motivating when you get good exam results. _____
3 You look very tired, Jessica. _____
4 How was the maths competition? _____
5 I'd like to do something positive this summer. _____
6 How was your walking holiday in Italy? _____
7 I think this homework project is tough. _____

A Yes, it is. Now I'm looking forward to starting my new course in September.
B Yes, it is, but if we do it together it will be easier.
C It was really challenging, but we won in the end.
D Yes, but tidying up at the end of it was exhausting. It took ages!
E I am. I need a relaxing holiday in the sun.
F Why don't you help at the children's summer camp? It's good experience.
G I loved it! It was a life-changing experience for me. I'm definitely going to spend more time in the mountains.

4 Choose the correct words.

A summer with a difference

In the summer I usually hang out with friends and have lots of 1) *tough/relaxing* days at the beach. However, this year I've decided to do something 2) *challenging/exhausting* in the holidays. I enjoy writing stories in my free time because it's 3) *life-changing/fun* so I've decided to do a creative writing course. Today was the first day. The first thing we had to do was stand up and talk about ourselves. I couldn't think what to say and my face went red! It was very 4) *embarrassing/motivating*! Then we wrote a poem which was really 5) *motivating/tough* because poems are difficult for me. But after we read them in class, the teacher said some very 6) *positive/embarrassing* things about mine. I was so happy.

5 Read the definitions and complete the phrasal verbs.

1	become something different	turn	*into*
2	start doing a new job or hobby	take	
3	stop doing something	give	
4	happen	take	
5	organise something	sort	
6	discover	find	
7	be involved in an event	take	
8	continue doing something	keep	

6 Choose the correct phrasal verbs.

1 We couldn't *find out/take part in* the price of the course so we didn't go.
2 Alice doesn't want to *keep on/give up* her English classes because they help her a lot.
3 I'm going to *take place/take part in* the school play because I love acting.
4 Can you *sort out/take up* the problem with this camera? I don't know what's wrong.
5 We've *given up/taken up* running because we want to get fit.
6 First the rain and now the snow. This picnic is *turning into/taking place* a disaster.

7 Choose the best answer, A, B or C.

1 I'm not going to _____ my drama class because I enjoy doing the shows.
  (A) give up   **B** keep on   **C** take up
2 It was _____ for Jack when he sent his email to the wrong person.
  A life-changing   **B** exhausting
  C embarrassing
3 A new first-aid course will _____ at the school this weekend.
  A take part in   **B** take place   **C** find out
4 I wanted to _____ the piano, but I couldn't find a teacher.
  A take up   **B** turn into   **C** keep on
5 Meeting the film director was _____ for Kate because he helped her become an actor.
  A relaxing   **B** challenging
  C life-changing
6 He used to be lazy, but he's _____ the best student in the class.
  A turned into   **B** sorted out   **C** given up

8 Complete the information with these adjectives and phrasal verbs.

> exhausting   find out   gave up
> is taking place   ~~keep on~~   positive
> take part in   tough

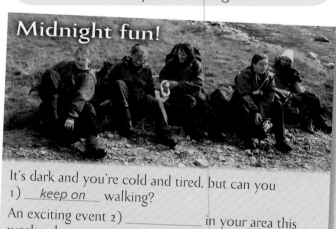

Midnight fun!

It's dark and you're cold and tired, but can you 1) *keep on* walking?

An exciting event 2) _____ in your area this weekend.

If you are between 14 and 18 years old, you can 3) _____ this night-time event. We're going to walk 20 km with expert guides to help us. It's long and 4) _____ so you will be tired, but you will make lots of new friends. Last year 100 people started the walk and 100 finished. Nobody 5) _____ and at the end they all said it was the most 6) _____ thing they had ever done.

If you're ready for this 7) _____ challenge and want to 8) _____ more, call 09847 84756.

GRAMMAR
Past perfect simple and past simple

1 Complete the sentences. Use the past perfect form of the verbs in brackets.

1 I _'d/had spoken_ (speak) to Sophie.
2 We _____ (not see) the film.
3 It _____ (not snow) for five years.
4 Did you think that Theo _____ (finish)?
5 He _____ (try) learning the guitar before.
6 James _____ (learn) something new.

2 Match the sentence beginnings (1–6) with the endings (A–F).

1 When I met Mark, _D_
2 The show began ___
3 After the party had finished, ___
4 We had just left a message for Anna ___
5 I had waited an hour for the bus ___
6 He didn't do the class ___

A they tidied up the house.
B when it finally came.
C because he had left his guitar at home.
D he had already started his course.
E when she arrived.
F before the girls had found their seats.

3 Choose the action that happens first in each sentence.

1 Alex and his friends decided *to go to the beach* after they *had finished studying*.
2 It *had been* warm all day, but it was very windy when *they arrived*.
3 They *sat* on the sand and ate the picnic that they *had prepared*.
4 Then they *went into the sea*, but they *hadn't noticed* the red flag.
5 Other swimmers *had left* the water, but Alex and Nathan *jumped* into the waves.
6 It *was difficult to swim* because the sea *had become* so wild.
7 Fortunately a life guard *had seen* them and he *called* to them to leave the water.
8 When they *got back* to their bags everybody else *had left* the beach.
9 They *were glad* the life guard *had helped* them.

4 Choose the correct words.

1 Sam's friends arrived before he *had eaten/ate* his breakfast.
2 The course had already started when Hannah *had decided/decided* to do it.
3 Last week I found a camera that somebody *had left/left* on the beach.
4 After Nick *had had/had* a few lessons, he began to cook for his friends.
5 A boy in Brazil *had called/called* Sonia because he had found her message in a bottle.
6 I *hadn't called/didn't call* you last night because I had had an exhausting day.
7 We were surprised when we heard that we *had won/won* the competition.
8 They *hadn't spent/didn't spend* all their money when they finished shopping.

5 Complete the article. Use the correct form of the verbs in brackets.

AN ARTISTIC SUMMER

Last summer I stayed with an aunt who 1) _had invited_ (invite) me to spend the school holidays with her. She 2) _____ (just / open) a summer school for young artists and asked me to help. I'd always got on well with her and 3) _____ (want) to go. The school had just started when I 4) _____ (arrive). Most of the students were between 14 and 18 and some of them 5) _____ (win) prizes for their art at school. Each day I 6) _____ (help) my aunt with the various activities that she had planned. One day I took a group of students to a park where some artists 7) _____ (arrange) an exhibition of huge sculptures. They were so cool. Before I stayed with my aunt I 8) _____ (not think) much about art. Now I can't wait to be one of her students.

6 Complete the magazine interview with the best answer, A, B or C, for each space.

	A		B		C	
1	A	've won	B	won	**C**	'd won
2	A	knew	B	know	C	've known
3	A	joined	B	'd joined	C	've joined
4	A	've done	B	'd done	C	do
5	A	'd heard	B	've heard	C	heard
6	A	had travelled	B	have travelled		
	C	has travelled				
7	A	'd made	B	make	C	've made
8	A	haven't tried	B	hadn't tried	C	didn't try

One lucky teenager from Turkey has just had a very exciting summer. Three months ago, Ali Gezmen won a competition for a place at a circus summer camp. So what was it like? At *Circus World* we went to find out.

CW: What did you think when you found out that you 1) *'d won* a place at the circus summer camp?

AG: I was really surprised. I 2) _____ that a lot of people had entered the competition. I didn't think I'd win.

CW: Had you had any experience of circus skills before you 3) _____ the summer camp?

AG: I 4) _____ a short course in juggling, but I wasn't very good.

CW: When did you decide to enter the competition?

AG: Well, I'd seen the circus a few times and then one day I 5) _____ about the summer camp on the radio.

CW: What were the other students like, Ali?

AG: They were really nice. Some of them 6) _____ a long way for the camp.

CW: Did you miss your friends and family at home?

AG: Yes, I did, but after I 7) _____ a few new friends I was fine.

CW: What was the best thing about the circus summer camp?

AG: I learned something new. I 8) _____ unicycling before I did the summer camp and now I'm mad about it!

CW: Thanks Ali.

LISTENING

1 🔊 **12.1** Listen to the start of a radio programme. Choose what Sophie is going to talk about.

1 Local news
2 Local music
3 Local events

2 🔊 **12.2** Listen to the rest of the radio programme. Complete the notes.

Art class with Nick Finley from the comic
1) _____WIZARD_____ , 10 until 2) _____
Five-a-side competition at the 3) _____
4) _____ stadium Cost: 5) £ _____
Whiteside Shopping Centre – new 6) _____
7) _____ until 9 p.m.!
Bus 8) _____ leaves from the 9) _____
10) _____ every half hour
Tonight in the town square – 11) _____
12) _____ with local music.

GRAMMAR
have/get something done

1 Write the words in the correct order to make sentences.

1 has / her / She / hair / cut / Paul / by / .
   She has her hair cut by Paul.

2 this afternoon / I / to / my / get / bike / want / repaired / .

3 do / eyes / you / your / Where / tested / have / ?

4 my / I'm / invitations / printed / having / .

5 not / I'm / getting / coloured / my / hair / .

6 checked / We / the / must / get / computer / .

2 Complete the sentences. Use the present simple or present continuous of *have/get* and the correct form of the verb in brackets.

1 I _have/get_ my teeth _checked_ every year. (check)

2 They often _____ their skateboards _____ in the shop. (repair)

3 Emma _____ her photo _____ at the moment. (take)

4 Daniel always _____ his hair _____ by his dad. (cut)

5 Where _____ your costumes _____? (you / make)

6 We _____ the classrooms _____ this year. (not paint)

SPEAKING SKILLS

1 Read the sentences (1–6). Choose if they are talking about experiences (E), situations now (N) or future plans (F).

1 I usually go shopping with my friends at the weekend. _N_

2 The camping trip to the mountains was fun. _____

3 I hope to work in a circus one day. _____

4 We enjoyed performing but it was exhausting. _____

5 I'm going to learn sign language. _____

6 Twice a week I visit my grandparents. _____

2 Put the words in the correct order to make sentences.

1 going / learn / to / I'm / year. / next / Chinese
   I'm going to learn Chinese next year.

2 was / library. / embarrassing / very / when / mobile / It / rang / in / my / the
   _____

3 the / life-changing / for / Winning / singing / was / James. / competition
   _____

4 to / train / relaxing. / Scotland / The / be / journey / very / can
   _____

5 swim / going / day. / to / across / that / I'm / river / one
   _____

6 km / taking / We're / race / part / in / a / 10 / today.
   _____

WRITING

1 Match (1–7) with (a–g) to complete the sentences of a story.

1 On my birthday last year _d_

2 The first thing we did was _____

3 After that we decided to swim _____

4 While we were swimming _____

5 Suddenly it started _____

6 After we had swum in the rain _____

7 At the end of the day we agreed _____

a we danced on the boat. It was brilliant.

b eat our picnic because we were starving.

c because it was incredibly hot.

d I went on a boat trip with some friends.

e that we had had a great time.

f to rain, but it was warm rain.

g we noticed some huge black clouds.

2 Complete the notes for a plan of a story. Use these phrases.

> drama club   ~~in the school holidays~~
> evening/saw where Narnia was filmed
> morning/visited castle   Prague, school trip
> afternoon/visited Barrandov film studio

1 When did the story take place?
   in the school holidays

2 Where did you go, and why? _____

3 Who did you go with? _____

4 What did you do first? _____

5 What other things did you do? _____

6 What did you do in the evening? _____

3 Read the magazine competition. Write your story. Remember to have a clear beginning, middle and end.

Do you have a story about a school trip?

Who were you with? What happened? How did it end? We want to hear all about it. Write about 100 words.

Revision Units 11 – 12

VOCABULARY

1 Complete the postcard with natural world words. The first letter has been given.

Hi Anna

I'm having a brilliant time in Cuba. After the bad
1) s _torm_ last night with rain and wind, today the
weather is great with lots of 2) s_____ .
There isn't a 3) c_____ in the sky.
The hotel is on the top of a 4) c_____ and
the views are amazing. Behind the hotel there's a
5) p_____ that you can walk down to the
beach. The sea is an incredible colour and the
6) s_____ is soft and white. This afternoon
we hope to go surfing because there are some great
7) w_____ .

See you soon

Max

2 Complete the sentences with the adjectives in brackets in the correct order.

1 They were going back to their tent when they saw some _____big black_____ clouds. (black/big)
2 We put our towels down on the _____ sand. (smooth/white)
3 I don't want to watch another _____ film. (old/boring)
4 They ate all of that _____ cake. (lovely/strawberry)
5 The children were drawing _____ stars on the wall. (yellow/small)
6 In the moon they could see the face of a(n) _____ man. (old/funny)

3 Complete the blog with these adjectives.

challenging   embarrassing   exhausting
~~fun~~   positive   relaxing

💬 View previous comments   Cancel   Share   Post

My first camping trip in the mountains and I'm
really enjoying it. I never knew camping could be
1) _____fun_____ ! The journey here took four hours,
but it was 2) _____ because we chatted and
listened to music. Unfortunately poor Charlie was
sick and the coach had to stop at the side of the
road. It was so 3) _____ for him! When we
arrived we had an 4) _____ two-hour walk
up the mountain to the campsite. Everybody was
tired and then we had to put up the tents. Some of
us didn't know how to do it. The teachers said that
this trip would be 5) _____ for us because
we come from the city. Some of us have never
camped before. However, with the teachers' help,
I think this will be a really 6) _____ week for
us all.

Write a comment   Support

4 Rewrite the sentences. Use a phrasal verb to replace the underlined words.

1 It was a long exhausting walk, but nobody <u>stopped</u>.
   It was a long exhausting walk, but nobody gave up.
2 A big party will <u>happen</u> on the last night of the camping trip.
   ....
3 I don't want this holiday to <u>become</u> a disaster.
   ....
4 Let's <u>discover</u> how much the trip costs.
   ....
5 Alice is going to <u>organise</u> the tickets and the travel arrangements.
   ....
6 Do you want to <u>continue</u> with your piano lessons?
   ....

GRAMMAR

1 **Complete the passive sentences. Use *by* where necessary.**

1 They take photos on the last day of school.
Photos ___are taken___ on the last day of school.

2 The students performed a musical.
A musical _____ the students.

3 They give the best student a prize.
A prize _____ to the best student.

4 The students don't take the books home.
The books _____ home.

5 They don't wear uniforms on the last day.
Uniforms _____ on the last day.

6 They make plans for the summer.
Plans _____ for the summer

7 The teachers prepare a party.
A party _____ the teachers.

8 One of the students filmed a video.
A video _____ one of the students.

2 **Complete the conversation. Use the past perfect or past simple form of the verbs in brackets.**

Hannah: Hi, Sam, you look fed up.

Sam: I am. I 1) _____*went*_____ (go) into town this morning with Gemma because we 2) _____ (arrange) to do a babysitting course. Gemma had seen an advert for it online and we 3) _____ (like) the idea.

Hannah: So what happened?

Sam: When we got there the course 4) _____ (start). The teacher said that the course was full and we couldn't join.

Hannah: 5) _____ (you / already / book) a place?

Sam: Yes, we had and we 6) _____ (call) to confirm the place after we'd sent the money.

Hannah: So what happened?

Sam: There was a mistake on their computer. They 7) _____ (not book) Gemma and me on a babysitting course. They 8) _____ (book) us on a course in flower arranging and we didn't want to do that!

3 **Write the words in the correct order to make sentences.**

1 could / your / old / You / clothes / recycle / .
You could recycle your old clothes.

2 we / shop / should / Maybe / to / another / go / ?
_____

3 You / his / use / phone / shouldn't / .
_____

4 try / Should / different / we / a / path / ?
_____

5 shouldn't / You / there / bag / leave / your / .
_____

6 We / stars / the / watch / tonight / could / .
_____

4 **Write sentences. Use *have/get* and the tenses in brackets.**

1 Jessica / her dress / make / for the school party. (present continuous)
Jessica is getting/having her dress made for the school party.

2 We / our eyes / check / every year. (present simple)
_____

3 The students / their exams / mark / now (present continuous)
_____

4 you / the room / decorate / for the event? (present continuous)
_____

5 I / never / my photo / take / in the morning. (present simple)
_____

6 They / the food and drinks / deliver / to the festival. (present simple)
_____

Exam information

The *Cambridge English Preliminary for Schools* exam is made up of three papers, each testing a different area of ability in English. The Reading and Writing paper is worth 50 per cent of the marks; the Listening paper is worth 25 per cent and the Speaking component is worth 25 per cent. There are five grades. A, B and C are pass grades; D and E are fail grades.

Reading and Writing (1 hour 30 minutes)

Reading		
Part 1 **Multiple choice**	*Focus*	Reading real-world notices, signs, postcards and other short texts for the main message
	Task	You read five separate short texts and answer multiple choice questions on each one, choosing from three options.
Part 2 **Matching**	*Focus*	Reading several texts for specific information and detailed comprehension
	Task	You read and match five descriptions of people to eight short texts.
Part 3 **True/False**	*Focus*	Processing a factual text and scanning it for specific relevant information
	Task	You read ten statements. You then read a longer factual text to decide whether each of the ten statements is correct or not.
Part 4 **Multiple choice**	*Focus*	Reading a text for detailed comprehension, and understanding the attitude, opinion and purpose of the writer
	Task	You read a longer text and answer five multiple choice questions, each with four options.
Part 5 **Multiple-choice cloze**	*Focus*	Understanding vocabulary and grammar in a short text
	Task	You read a factual or narrative text with ten gaps. You choose the correct word to fill each gap from four options.
Writing		
Part 1 **Sentence transformations**	*Focus*	Knowledge of vocabulary and understanding of grammatical sentence structure
	Task	You read five pairs of sentences linked in theme, and complete the second sentence in each pair so that it has the same meaning as the first sentence. You should not write more than three words for each sentence.
Part 2 **Short communicative message**	*Focus*	Communicating three specific points in a short message, such as a postcard, note or email
	Task	You follow instructions given in the task and write a short communicative message. There are three points in the instructions that you must include in your message. You should write 35–45 words.
Part 3 **Longer piece of continuous writing**	*Focus*	Control and range of language in continuous text
	Task	You choose to write either an informal letter or a story, using about 100 words.

Listening (approximately 30 minutes)

Part 1	Focus	Listening to identify key information
Multiple choice	Task	You listen to seven short monologues or dialogues and look at three pictures for each one. You choose the correct picture for each answer.
Part 2	Focus	Listening to identify specific information and detailed meaning
Multiple choice	Task	You listen to a longer monologue or interview. There are six questions. You choose the correct answer for each question from three options.
Part 3	Focus	Listening to identify, understand and interpret information
Gap fill	Task	You read notes or sentences with six gaps. You listen to a longer monologue and fill in the missing information.
Part 4	Focus	Listening for detailed meaning, and to identify the attitudes and opinions of speakers
True/False	Task	You read six statements. You then listen to an informal dialogue and decide whether the statements are true or false.

Speaking (approximately 10–12 minutes)

Part 1	Focus	Giving factual and personal information
Examiner-led conversation	Task	The examiner asks you and your partner short questions in turn for 2–3 minutes.
Part 2	Focus	Making and responding to suggestions, discussing alternatives and making recommendations
Simulated situation	Task	You and your partner are given a task to discuss together for 2–3 minutes, with visuals to help you. You should negotiate and reach a decision.
Part 3	Focus	Describing photographs using appropriate vocabulary, and organising an extended turn
Individual extended turn	Task	You and your partner are each given a photograph to describe. You speak alone for about 1 minute.
Part 4	Focus	Expressing opinions, likes/dislikes, preferences, experiences, etc.
General conversation	Task	You and your partner talk to each other for about 3 minutes. The examiner gives you a task to discuss that is linked in theme to the pictures you described in Part 3.

NOTES

NOTES

NOTES

NOTES

NOTES

NOTES

Pearson Education Limited
Edinburgh Gate
Harlow
Essex CM20 2JE
England
and Associated Companies throughout the world.

www.english.com/goldxp

© Pearson Education Limited 2016

The right of Jill Florent and Suzanne Gaynor to be identified as authors of this Work has been asserted by them in accordance with the Copyright, Designs and Patents Act 1988.

First published 2016
Third impression 2018

ISBN: 9781292159478

Set in 10pt Mixage ITC Std
Printed by Neografia in Slovakia

Acknowledgements
The publishers and author would like to thank the following people for their feedback and comments during the development of the material:

Elif Berk, Turkey; Alan Del Castillo Castellanos, Mexico; Dilek Kokler, Turkey; Trevor Lewis, The Netherlands; Nancy Ramirez, Mexico; Jacqueline Van Mil-Walker, The Netherlands

The publisher would like to thank the following for their kind permission to reproduce their photographs:

(Key: b-bottom; c-centre; l-left; r-right; t-top)

123RF.com: 73, 78, Markus Mainka 71, Viewapart 7b; **Alamy Images:** Alexander Caminada 75t, Bernadette Delaney 47br, CountrySideCollection - Homer Sykes 82, Cultura RM 56bl, Dennis MacDonald 47cl, Directphoto.org 22b, incamerastock 53cl, Jeff Greenberg 84, Judith Collins 41t, Lebrecht Music and Arts Photo Library 13cl, PhotoAlto 47tr, Radius Images 87, Steve Gottlieb 55, tbkmedia.de 41b; **Corbis:** Daniel Munoz / Reuters 6b, Ocean 12; **DK Images:** Alex Robinson 83, Andy Crawford 61tl, Gary Ombler 61tr, Linda Burgess 61bl, Nikid Design Ltd 61cr, Trish Gant 47cr; **Fotolia.com:** Akbudak Rimma 47bc, Alehdats 61cl, Alex Starseltsev 64tl, biglama 64bl, Corinaldo 53br, Costin79 49cr/C, Orcea David 49cl/A, Dmitry 21tl/1A, Faabi 35cl, fotomaster 64bc, Andrey Gontarenko 80tl, Joe Gough 21br/5C, indigolotos 21cl/3A, Alex Ishchenko 64br, Gail Johnson 37, kmiragaya 21/4B, Patryk Kosmider 21/2A, M.studio 21bl/5A, mdb 38, Okinawakasawa 61br, Piotr Pawinski 21tc/1B, 21tr/1C, Pshenichka 21/2C, Raywoo 41c, rydrych 21cr/3C, solovyova 80tr, Nikolai Sorokin 21/4C, vetkit 49c/B, wolfelarry 21/2B; **Getty Images:** Dori OConnell 69, Matthew Lloyd 45; **MIXA Co., Ltd:** 63bl; **Pearson Education Ltd:** Studio 8 30, 39, Martin Beddall 18t, Jörg Carstensen 23, 32cr, Stuart Cox 66, Gareth Boden 16c, 32cl, Handan Erek 16tl, Jon Barlow 16tr, 16b, 32t, 32b, 78cr, Jules Selmes 18b, 52t, 52br; **PhotoDisc:** John A. Rizzo 12b; **Rex Shutterstock:** APA 53tl; **Shutterstock.com:** 35cr, bayberry 9, bikeriderlondon 47bl, BlueSkyImage 11b, Boleslaw Kubica 21bc/5B, Dmitry Berkut 53cr, Dmitry Kolmakov 64tr, ElenaGaak 13cr, Galina Barskaya 14, 29, Giuseppe_R. 15, Kruglov_Orda 19, Lenetstan 49tl, Markus Mainka 53tr, Eugenio Marongiu 46, Monticello 64tc, Moreno Soppelsa 21c/3B, Paul Hakimata Photography 52c, Pavel L Photo and Video 80tc, Pavel Svoboda 79, Peresanz 63tr, Roger Jegg - Fotodesign-Jegg.de. 52b, Simone van den Berg 13b, Slavoljub Pantelic 56bl, Stokkete 48, Stuart Monk 59b, Lee Torrens 38c, Tyler Olson 75b, Vaclav Volrab 81, Vectomart 50br, viki2win 47tl, Wavebreakmedia 33, Whitelook 53bl, YanLev 25; **SuperStock:** Age fotostock 77, Marka 86; **Veer / Corbis:** LCS 21/4A

Illustrated by: Caron Painter (Sylvie Poggio) 67; Andrew Painter 7, 27; Ned Woodman 4, 5; Niall Harding (Beehive Illustration) 28, 49, 50, 64

Cover images: *Front:* **Fotolia.com:** Alexander Yakovlev

All other images © Pearson Education

Every effort has been made to trace the copyright holders and we apologise in advance for any unintentional omissions. We would be pleased to insert the appropriate acknowledgement in any subsequent edition of this publication.